Teaching local history

W B Stephens

Manchester University Press

© W. B. Stephens 1977

Published by
Manchester University Press
Oxford Road
Manchester M13 9PL

ISBN 0 7190 0660 0

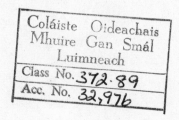
Printed in Great Britain
at the Alden Press, Oxford

Contents

Illustrations

Author's note

This book is not intended for those who wish to pursue original research into local history—they might find my *Sources for English Local History*, Manchester University Press, 1973, useful for their purposes. Rather is it written for use by teachers in junior, middle, and secondary schools and for student teachers. It outlines the case for the inclusion of local history in the school curriculum, notes the theoretical and practical implications and difficulties involved, and seeks to show at a practical level what can be done. Particular stress is laid on the use of primary source material, since, while it is now generally acknowledged that the source approach is an essential part of historical training at all levels, and is invaluable for integrated and environmental studies, no really detailed guide at school level has so far been available. I think that the work will be useful, too, for those who teach in further and adult education, though that is not its prime intention.

In the allotted space I have not been able to deal with every topic I would like to have included, but I hope that enough significant aspects are covered to make this a worthwhile reference book both as to materials and ideas for their use. I have not presumed to fill precious pages with instructions on such matters as what work cards are and how they should be compiled, what is meant by dramatic work, imaginative exercises, modelling and so on, for teachers of history and other subjects will already be familiar with those terms and well grounded in such methods, while for students in training there are plenty of manuals to help them with such basic matters.

I have tried not to be too fanciful or ambitious in my suggestions for pupils' activities, and I have attempted to show how local history, and in particular local history source material, can be used both in more and in less traditional syllabuses, in syllabuses attuned mainly to national and general history as well as in those centred on local and environmental studies. While I draw attention to many kinds of useful manuscript sources, I have had in mind the teacher's need for accessible material and I have therefore laid much emphasis on types of material which are available in print. In the notes I have given references to detailed accounts by teachers and others of relevant school activities and experiments.

Thus I hope that those who wish to use local history with their pupils will be assisted by this book. They will, however, need to look on it as a basis and a stimulus, for its message is that successful teachers in this area,

x   *Author's note*

as in others, need to put in some hard work (individually or in groups), in libraries, record offices, and in the field.

My thanks are due to my colleagues at the University of Leeds, Dr Paul Sharp and Dr Robert Unwin, who were good enough to read drafts of certain chapters. The volume has benefited from their comments, but, of course, the responsibility for the views expressed remains mine. I am grateful, too, to Mr Philip Mays for providing the photographs of children working on Sandal Castle excavations; to pupils at West Leeds Girls' High School, Lawnswood School, Leeds, and Royston Church of England School, Barnsley, for illustrative material; and to various publishers, editors and record societies, whose permission to reproduce record material is indicated in the Bibliographical Notes. And I am also indebted to the numerous schoolteachers I have consulted for their useful comments, and for keeping my feet where those of every good local historian should be, on the ground. Finally I should like to record my thanks to the officers of the Manchester University Press for their careful assistance at the publication stage.

W. B. S.

Haske
Crediton
August 1976

1 Local history and its value in school

The increase in popular interest in history since the Second World War is evidenced by the demand in bookshops and libraries for biographies and works on political, social, local and other aspects of history, by the popularity of films and television series concerned with history, architecture and archaeology, and of fictional drama in historical settings. Increased leisure combined with the motor-car and foreign travel has made visits to historic sites and buildings and to museums and exhibitions more and more common. Moreover people generally are becoming aware that current economic, social and political situations are unintelligible without an understanding of the historical background.

It is perhaps strange that in these circumstances history in school has not in recent years proved popular. While at the university and college levels there is no shortage of history students and while the subject is still one of the main GCE A level choices, beneath the sixth form there is no great enthusiasm for the subject, particularly among those who leave school at sixteen. Mary Price, in a now famous article, drew attention to a survey made in 1966 of the opinions of some 10,000 of such girls and boys, who placed history at the bottom of the list of 'useful and interesting subjects' and very high in the list of 'useless and boring subjects'. History, she pointed out, was in danger not only of losing the battle 'for its place in the curriculum, but for a place in the minds and interests of the young'.[1]

It is not difficult to suggest reasons why history, so attractive to adults, is apparently so uninteresting to children today. In the first place history teachers have been trained largely in political history, and the school syllabus still often reflects this emphasis. Yet much political history, especially when concerned with constitutional issues and foreign policy, is treated in an abstract and theoretical fashion, intellectually and emotionally remote, and inappropriate to the conceptual abilities of many children, and particularly of the average child below sixteen.

Nor has it proved a sufficient remedy to replace the political emphasis by one on social and economic history. Too often the teacher, himself untrained in these aspects of history, draws his knowledge from elementary textbooks, many of them outdated and lacking in interest, and does not possess the background of intimate knowledge needed to clothe the textbook skeleton and bring it to life. Moreover the content of social and economic history has drawbacks. It frequently lacks the great man and the exciting incident that political history can provide, and some of the more important concepts of economic history can be more abstract and difficult to understand than those of political history. Fiscal reform and the development of free trade, for example, are likely to be more abstract, less interesting and harder to comprehend than parliamentary reform or the Indian mutiny. And, taught at a more elementary level, social history has a tendency to degenerate into classroom antiquarianism. The study of costume may be cited as an example. Many teachers concern themselves here with no more than 'What did people wear at the time?' To turn this antiquarianism into history requires tackling with the pupils such problems as 'Why did people wear clothes like this at the time?' 'Why did some people wear quite different costumes to others?' 'Why did one fashion give way to another?' and so on. Moreover, concentration on economic and social history can give as one-sided an outlook on the past as an exclusive concern with political and constitutional affairs. And it might be argued that though political history has often been treated in a colourless and abstract way this is by no means a necessity, and that since politics is so much a part of life the future voter must be introduced to it in the schoolroom in however elementary a way.

As well as the content, teaching methods must share the blame for the boredom engendered by many history lessons. Too often real history has been betrayed by its reduction to the handing down of a catalogue of accepted facts: dictated notes, learning by rote, and regurgitation; lessons that always follow the same pattern, the teacher lecturing, the children absorbing, sponge-like. The danger of such methods and the vital need for variety have long been accepted by history teachers in theory but too often ignored in practice.

Perhaps equally significant is the immeasurable but clearly evident decline in the confidence of history teachers, young and old, in the value of their own subject. There is grudging admission that other, newer subjects deriving from the social sciences—such as environmental studies and social studies—primarily concerned with clearly relevant present-day issues, must be more 'useful' to the child. Professor Burston has exposed the weaknesses of the anti-intellectual heresy that the understanding of present society and preparation for membership of it are best achieved by a direct study of the mechanics of that society, with history playing a subsidiary part or no part at all,[2] but it still has strong advocates, whose philistinism in this respect must be regretted, but into whose hands uninspired history teaching plays.

Since Mary Price's article appeared, however, much has been done to strengthen the position of history in school and to improve its value and attractiveness to pupils. Those professionally concerned with history teaching at school level have placed much faith in the potential of two aspects of the subject in sponsoring revival—contemporary world history, and local history. Contemporary history has disadvantages as well as advantages, but to the child at any rate it appears more obviously relevant to the present and its advocates claim is more successful in engendering interest than the study of earlier periods. It allows the use of such attractive teaching materials as photographs and films, and presents the possibility of contact at first or second hand with those still alive who have lived through the years and events being studied. And there is copious source material, readily available and easily legible. Contemporary world history thus gives on the one hand the broad sweep of international macro-history, if you like, and on the other the cosiness of chronological nearness to the life of the child and his family.

The nature and standing of local history

The other prong of the historians' counter-attack has been the development of local history, to provide, shall we say, the micro-history to offset or complement the broad sweep, and to embrace the spatial nearness of the child's environment. Combined with this have been serious attempts to strengthen the part played by history, particularly local history, in the growth of schemes of integrated or related studies. In all these developments there has been evidence of a determination on the one hand to increase opportunities for variety in activity and presentation, and on the other to introduce children to the way historians think and work and the way history comes to be written, and to develop those skills which a proper study of history involves. Changes in the nature and standing of local history at an adult level have made it a subject much worthier of consideration as a significant ingredient of school study than it once

was. For long English local history was hag-ridden by its past antiquarianism and its attraction for well intentioned but often undisciplined amateurs, and as recently as 1952 H. P. R. Finberg, the first
professor of local history appointed by a British university, could
describe his subject as 'the Cinderella among historical studies'.
Since then, however, local history has not only carved out for itself a
respectable place in the academic world but has also become acceptable to a new generation of well informed amateurs. The coincidence
of the expansion of undergraduate and postgraduate studies in
history and the social sciences with the greater availability of local
records has encouraged teaching and research in many aspects of local
history. Much national history, especially social and economic history,
has been rewritten or reinterpreted in the light of local research, and
the continual investigation of local history as a necessary basis for a
more accurate and fuller general history is now largely accepted. But,
mainly as a result of the efforts of the school of local historians connected with or influenced by the department of English Local
History at Leicester University, local history has emerged also as a
disciplined academic study in its own right rather than as merely an
ancillary to national history. Professors Hoskins and Finberg have
developed a rationale to justify this extension. They admit that the
history of any locality, town or parish, county or region, forms part of
and shares in national history, in the same way as British history is
part of European or of world history. Yet, they argue, each place also
has its own history, just as English history is distinct from European
history. Local history is not merely national history writ small. What
was important locally was not necessarily significant nationally, and
local history is more the history of those matters that differed
regionally than of those which were the same. Whatever each area
and place in the past shared with others, it also had different experiences, particularly in the realms of economic and social change, and
it is in these fields that the peculiar localness of local history is especially evident.

Because, moreover, each area has its own historical experience, its
purely local history has a time scale of its own which does not
necessarily coincide with the time scale of national history. Chronological periods at local level may be determined partly by national
events, but they are often also determined by local ones, and the high-
lights and the depressions will differ in one part of the country from
those in another. Professor Finberg, in a now well-known formula,
has defined the task of the local historian as the study of 'the Origin,

Growth, Decline, and Fall of a Local Community', though, of course, any particular community will not necessarily have passed through all these stages. If undertaken properly, using the highly sophisticated techniques worked out in recent years and with a sound background knowledge of general history, the study of local history is a worthwhile pursuit which does not now need to justify its existence solely as a provider of some of the grains making up the sand dune of national history.

Because it is concerned with change in the locality it is particularly interested in the structure of the local society—the whole community, not merely the ruling class—the occupational structure, the demographic structure, the social structure, and in the economic basis—in particular local industry, trade and farming. To these are related the topography of the locality, its communication system and those aspects of local government and politics that did not merely reflect the national story.

Another function of local history has recently been stressed—its value for purposes of comparative study.[3] Though different communities had different historical experiences, some had much in common with others, and it is a proper extension of local history to seek to classify types of locality for different purposes, to show what, for example, industrial communities had in common in the eighteenth century, and how aspects of life in them, such as religious persuasion, may have differed from those in market towns, or rural villages. It is important to try to explain why some communities had different experiences from others—not only why or how a rural village differed from an industrial town, but why the experience of one industrial town was not the same as that of another. In a sense this approach points to the artificiality of the very concept of a national picture of society in many aspects of life before the present century.

We are thus now far removed from the day when many professional historians saw local history merely as the parochial reflection of national history or as an amusement for the amateur. Moreover the combination of the increasing availability of source material and the emergence of a large group of young professionals trained in the techniques of local historical research has resulted in the publication of a body of books and articles the scholarly level of which is as high as in other branches of history. At the same time there has been an upsurge of popular interest in the subject. Here much credit must be given to W. G. Hoskins, who in such books as *The Making of the English Landscape* (1955) and *Local History in England* (1959; 1972) (the latter specifically written 'not for the specialist or the professional historian' but 'for the great army of amateurs in this field') has provided popular scholarly work and guidance which have been a revelation and an inspiration to many.

The purpose of local history in school

It is with the part local history can play in the reshaping of historical studies in school that this book is concerned. It may, of course, be argued that history teachers have for long been encouraged to use local history in their lessons and that for generations many have in fact done so. There is some truth in this. In some areas, for example, certain aspects of local history can hardly be ignored—as, for example, the growth in Lancashire of the cotton industry. But even in such cases it is surprising how often the principle is accepted but the chance ignored.

In the decade or so before the outbreak of the First World War both the Historical Association and the new Board of Education urged on teachers the educational value of using local history in their lessons.[4] The stress then and for long since has been on the value of local history as a colourful means of illustrating national history. Thus Professor Hearnshaw wrote in 1908, 'of course, we all agree that local history must be used in a way entirely subsidiary', and refers to it as 'a storehouse of vivid and pregnant illustration of the general course of national history'.[5] In 1929 the orthodox view was still that 'local history is not as a first introduction to the past, but for illustration at every stage',[6] and more recently W. H. Burston, in 1963, strongly urged that 'what is required from local history, ideally, is local illustration of national themes and development'.[7] Now, however, just as in the more academic reaches of higher education and historical research, there is a growing feeling that there is a place for the historical study of the locality in its own right.[8]

What attitude should the teacher take to these two viewpoints? Is he to accept fully the traditional view that local history should be used to illustrate national views by providing apposite examples? Or is he to pay some attention to the claim that the uniqueness of the history of the child's own region merits some attention? My answer can represent only a personal viewpoint. On the whole I would consider the history teacher, or the school, which allows its pupils to complete their school life without a general knowledge of national development in the context of wider historical change to have failed to provide them with an important part of basic education. Those who are, for example, in however hazy and elementary a way, unaware of the development of British parliamentary democracy, or the rise and fall of empires, of the industrial revolution, of the impact and nature of wars, of Cromwell, Napoleon, Hitler or Stalin and many other significant historical themes, events and personages, must be considered culturally deprived. Such content in history teaching, despite what many educationists may propose, is important. Detailed knowledge of the development of the West Riding woollen industry is not directly part of the general cultural heritage and is no substitute for it. Thus I would support the view that the best use of local history will often be as an ancillary to the teaching of general history. But this should be interpreted as including not only the traditional inclusion of illustrative examples but also the use of local material to introduce themes or topics to be studied at national or international level. In the following chapters, therefore, I have devoted much space to suggestions to help teachers to use local history in their teaching of general history, for while many are anxious to do so they are frequently unsure where appropriate material is to be found and how it can be utilized.

Yet the history teacher would be doing a disservice both to his pupils and to his discipline if he were to give the impression that the history of their own locality was merely the history of England in miniature, any more than the history of England was the same as the history of France or the development of Russia identical with that of the United States. It has been argued that pupils may be confused if introduced to regional developments or events which run counter to the generalizations being taught regarding national history.[9] But while the danger of confusion must be kept in mind, it is surely part of historical training to recognize that generalizations are generalizations, that exceptions are always likely to be found, and in particular that there may be local variations. The use of local history only when local experience agrees with the national trends proclaimed by the textbook is to make the teacher guilty of oversimplification and indeed of purveying a distorted view of historical reality. Such a policy can lead to difficulties where pupils are themselves aware from outside reading of facts about their own locality. The Poor Law Amendment Act of 1834, for example, did not apply to Coventry, and to give Coventry children the impression that it did would be both improper and educationally unwise. Moreover regional developments which clearly greatly affected national development must not be treated in isolation. In real life the success story is only one side of experience. In the industrial revolution period Lancashire, Yorkshire and the Midlands were not Britain. The formerly thriving West Country cloth industry declined in the same period, and population there did not increase at a galloping rate. The one story is no more the national experience than the other.

There is room and indeed a need to teach local history also in its own right, to show how local differed from national history as well as how it conformed. The sensible teacher will seek to teach local history hand-in-hand and side-by-side with general history, pointing to the locality's sharing in national experiences and to its unique story. On the whole a comparative approach is best attempted, with the local set against the national and even against the international, and with local variations compared not only with the national norm but also with other local variations from that norm. Thus one would hope, for example, that the myth of the ubiquity of the three-field classical manor would no longer be taught and that medieval farming organization in Devon might be compared not only with that in the Midlands but with that in Wales, Norfolk and even other parts of Europe. The study of local castles, churches and monasteries might well be linked not only with the study of those in other parts of Britain but with those in Europe and Asia, too. Concern with local uniqueness should not lead to blinkered parochialism but be out-ward-looking. Local history should not, then, displace other aspects of history teaching in the school, but rather should add to and enrich the teaching of the subject as a whole.

Advantages of teaching local history

Since local history is properly part of general history, the reason for teaching it is an aspect of the reason for teaching history generally. Now the nature of history in school and elsewhere, and the purpose and value of its study, have been extensively examined in many books and continue to be debated. It is not possible here to treat this topic in any detail but it may be noted that important arguments for teaching history to children include the access it gives to that continually shifting body of knowledge of mankind in the past that permits the children to share in the common culture of the community. Related to this is the help it gives to the understanding of present society, both by demonstrating how that society has evolved and by con-trasting it with other societies in the past. And since society is composed of individuals, the development of disciplined imagination through the vicarious experience of individuals in the past can lead to some insight into the motivations, actions and beliefs of others. Study in depth of a complete society in the past can, moreover, teach the complexity of human life and relationships, and of social change and development. Such study, historians claim, is more valuable an introduction to real life than the models of the social scientists, who sometimes appear to examine unreal situations composed of selected factors (excluding other variables) and extrapolate from them with the saving *ceteris paribus* when any historian knows that other factors never remain the same.

Yet for an insight both into historical and present situations some appreciation of the techniques used by historians is needful. To answer the question commonly heard in school—How do we know?— is an important part of history teaching. It involves introducing children to such facets of historical work as the collection, analysis and evaluation of evidence, and it is with the development of skills related to these processes that teachers of history are becoming more concerned than they have previously been. Again, history teaching seeks to kindle an interest in the past not only for the reasons given above but also in order to give access to a vast intellectual area in which many adults find much enjoyment. If the stimulation of interest and enjoyment is not an integral part of all history teaching then the other benefits are unlikely to ensue.

It would be unrealistic to claim that these benefits are to be obtained best or only through the study of local history; but it is clear that local history can do much to increase the likelihood of the history teacher's success in achieving them. In the first place experience shows that local history is likely to interest many pupils of all ages and that a great number of children derive positive enjoyment from its study. It can be an antidote both to the boredom resulting from lack of variety of approach and to the seeming unreality that is often engendered by the sort of history that deals largely with generalized, and to the child, inert conclusions. It may, therefore, help to provide greater comprehension which is likely to bring greater enjoyment. Jacquetta Hawkes has claimed that 'there is no human being, I believe, who is not stirred by the places of his childhood', and May McKisack has stressed the powerful urge that may be engendered in children by 'their love of an old house, or town, or village . . . or listening to the tales of a grandfather'; these 'may awake them in youth to curiosity about the lives of their forbears and the different strands that have gone to their own make-up'.[10] If the teacher can harness this native attachment to a disciplined study of the locality it can lead to a lifelong interest both in local and in general history. Those who have used local history with children will be aware not only of this abiding enjoyment—which is often a long-term achievement—but of the immediate excitement and sense of adventure that many children can experience.

Local history can also complement the study of world and contemporary history, by providing study in depth. Not all 'broad sweep' history is superficial, but there is a tendency for trends to predominate over people, and local history can emphasize that real people in complex situations are the basis for historians' generalizations, and that generalizations blur differences and may depress the significance of the human element. The local war memorial and the state of affairs it recorded are not unrelated to the battlefields of France and Flanders in the First World War; and the topography of the centre of the city in which we live may have been affected by Marshal Goering as well as by Town Hall planners.

Again, local history has certain advantages which can help to break down the barriers between school and the world outside. In the first place, to stress the obvious, it deals with places the child knows and which are not merely—like Louis XIV's barrier fortresses—names on a map. Thus though the chronological gap remains, the spatial gap between the past and the world of the child is narrowed. The methods applied in the study of local history take the pupils out into their own district on fieldwork and visits, and bring to their notice records which relate to places they know. This is important, for the exclusive study of national politics and foreign policy can suggest to the young that history is 'just part of school', as unlikely to be of significance or interest to adults in the workaday world as square roots or irregular verbs. In pursuing local history, however, the child is brought into a fresh contact with adults, and the experiences of the elderly and the middle-aged, including his own relatives, become part and parcel of his historical study. Moreover pupils will become aware, by meeting archivists, archaeologists, museum curators, members of local historical societies and the like, that history is not merely what is printed in the textbook; it is an on-going business in which real people, professionals earning a living and others, not only teachers, are occupied and interested, and the pursuit of which exists apart from school.

Further pedagogical reasons also support the use of local history in school. Although an increasing amount of research is being undertaken into psychological aspects of history teaching, comparatively little of a conclusive nature has yet emerged from it to guide the practice of history teachers.[11] What has, however, appears to confirm the subjective conclusions of many history teachers over a long period—that most children throughout their school life, or at any rate below the sixth form, find abstract concepts difficult to comprehend. This suggests that the teacher should approach the abstract by means of the concrete and the general by the particular, and the opportunities offered for this by local history are, as we shall see, considerable. Use of the child's limited environment introduces immediately an element of concreteness, and local history provides, perhaps more than most traditional history, many kinds of activities, practical and more intellectual, involving contact with tangible and visible objects, materials and places.

Local history is valuable, too, in providing links between history and other subjects, and as an ingredient of integrated studies of one sort or another. Geography, environmental studies, social studies and civics all have an historical element, and often local history can play an important part in their teaching. Its greatest value, however, lies in what it can contribute to historical training.

Traditional academic grammar-school history teaching has not been as guilty as is sometimes inferred of ignoring the development of the historical processes of observation and discovery, collection and classification of evidence, deduction from the evidence, and presentation of conclusions. This has taken the form at best of the use of several textbooks, published collections of documents and books of reference as sources to gather information, the processing of this into some sort of pattern (as 'notes'), and further deductions presented as essays or exercises. Too often, however, the basic intentions of these methods have been forgotten, and history teaching takes the form of reading and copying from a single textbook. Moreover, rather than 'note-making', involving thought on the part of the pupil, we have 'note-taking' and the regurgitation of these dictated or copied notes as 'essays' into which no thought processes have entered. Even examination questions designed to stimulate thought and deduction, such as 'Why did Parliament win the Civil War?' are frequently thwarted by those who teach 'causes' and 'results' as sets of facts to be received from on high and committed to memory without thought. It is unfortunate that such a procedure often results in 'good' examination results, for it patently does not produce in schoolchildren any abiding interest in history or understanding of its nature.

An intelligent use of local history, however, can do much to help improve this state of affairs. It offers, for example, an opportunity of getting away from the textbook in a way more difficult in other aspects of history. For almost every area there is a wealth of interesting source material to be tapped, and this is so varied in nature that all ages and types of pupil can be catered for. Children of all age groups confronted with the raw materials of history of their own town can hardly fail to gain some glimmering of the nature of the historian's craft. With younger pupils the chief object is to make them aware of the existence of such things as documents and to show them that history concerns real events that occurred even in their own town. With older and more intelligent pupils the material can be used to give some idea of what historians do with such evidence.

Apart from printed and documentary source material in abundance, the local historian can provide, too, evidence of a kind unique as far as the child is concerned—the landscape itself (rural and urban) and the physical remains of man's activities in the past—houses, factories, public buildings, churches, schools, roads, canals, railways, abbeys, castles, archaeological sites and so on, as well as collections of physical objects in museums, and of archives in record offices. They can be related to intelligent library work of the kind that has long been advocated but not often undertaken, for children must learn that the past is not something to be discovered *in toto* from scratch. They must be made aware that secondary works are important and that historians advance knowledge not only by collecting fresh evidence but by standing on the shoulders of those who have gone before. This linking of source material with published works on national and local history and with reference books is essential if the way historians work is to be understood, and local history offers good opportunities for such work.

Moreover the nature of local history and its practice are such that it can be used successfully with pupils of different ages and varying abilities. It is particularly suitable for teaching mixed-ability classes, since the breadth of its content, embracing both the academic and the practical, provides opportunities for a multiplicity of approaches and activities. Though local history has more to offer the secondary-school pupil than the younger child, it nevertheless has a part to play in the junior school. Young children learn much through a study of their environment, building on what they know and understand. Many teachers of this age group therefore find that local history can play some part in the well tried concentric approach to learning, where the child progresses from the smaller circles of his environment to widening circles as increasing maturity permits. It has been shown, too, that junior-school children can profitably be introduced to historical methodology and that work with documents accords with recent views on how children learn.[12]

In deprived downtown areas and with backward children it is less a case of building on what is known of the locality and relating it to national and international history than of using local history as an introduction to the town in which they live and of which they have usually a very restricted knowledge.

Much local history can be presented in a non-literary fashion by the use of visual and physical materials, and fieldwork and visits, themselves outdoor pursuits, can lead on in school to activities of a practical nature such as model, plan and map construction, drawings and sketches, dramatic work and displays. The practical side of local history can be attractive and educationally successful with children generally, but particularly with those in the age range five to thirteen and with those older children with a non-literary bent to whom a strong visual and practical impact is essential.[13] The aspect of novelty may well also excite the interest of the growing number of non-academic sixth formers. To them fieldwork, archaeology, vernacular architecture and aspects of recent local history—all very worthwhile subjects of study—can prove attractive. In many cases they will bring the pupils into contact with the outside world and provide stimulating activities of a practical kind.

There is, however, a rigorously academic side to local history, and many children of average ability and above will benefit from acquaintance with this. Much in the following chapters will show how local history can be made use of in traditional syllabuses as well as in new approaches at an intellectual level. Opportunities for bringing it into external examination at the sixteen-plus level already exist. If less specialized A level examinations or an extended CSE are instituted, local history as a subject in its own right may prove worthwhile and attractive, for it would in many cases be a fresh subject and not a mere continuation of earlier school work.

Finally it may be that local history can help to satisfy the apparently increasing need felt by people today to identify themselves with groups smaller than the national. A large number of children in an era of mobility of labour, of the destruction of old communities and the erection of new towns, new estates and new schools, find themselves intellectually and emotionally bereft of roots. At worst they are attracted to gangs, but many thirst for the security of belonging to a comprehensible group of which they can be proud. They are, then, potentially interested in their own town and their own county. The history teacher may use local history to reveal the antiquity, uniqueness and complexity of the community in which the child lives and so strengthen the sense of belonging to something that transcends the present. The sense of time and continuity that can be comprehended perhaps most easily at the local level in the study of the past can lead to an appreciation of the significance and value of history generally, for no one would wish the results of all this to be the engendering of parish-pump insularity.

For notes to this chapter see p. 164.

2 Theoretical and practical problems

Those who are concerned to maintain a balance between a history syllabus that is interesting, attractive and appropriate to their pupils' stages of intellectual development, and history teaching that is intellectually demanding and academically respectable, may well have mixed feelings about a too facile acceptance of local history into the school curriculum, and there are certain problems to be faced. It has been argued, for example, that local history is by no means an elementary aspect of its parent discipline. Indeed, H. P. R. Finberg has claimed that 'in its higher reaches it demands mature scholarship and a wide background of general culture', and suggests, too, that to treat local history as introductory or contributory to national history is to invert the true relationship. Only 'when we are thoroughly grounded in the history of England: then and not till then can we begin to think of writing the history of Liverpool, or Lydiard Millicent or Saffron Waldon'.

It would indeed be difficult for any advanced study to be undertaken by anyone who was ignorant of the context of national history within which local events and developments occurred. He would not be able to judge whether aspects of regional history were on the one hand typical and merely what was happening everywhere, or, on the other, peculiar to that place; nor would he be able to take into account the reasons for changes the impetus for which may have derived from events outside the locality. Local history, despite its uniqueness, cannot be understood in a vacuum, any more than British history can be comprehended without reference to European or extra-European history. Again it is more difficult for the local historian than for the scholar who works at the national level to confine his attentions to a single chronological period. The local field of study is narrower in the topographical sense, but at that level the student is more frequently brought up against the continuity of history and is forced to be interested in developments across long periods of time. This combination of a need for considerable knowledge of national and even international history with the need to straddle the years from say the medieval period or before to the twentieth century, and the further requirement to be interested in a rounded view of history—social and economic in particular, but political and ecclesiastical too—does indicate that the successful adult local historian must have a considerable and diverse background of historical knowledge. To this may be added the need for a topographical sense and a nodding acquaintance with geology, archaeology and place-name studies, and with the tools of palaeography and medieval Latin. Moreover the field is one in which textbooks hardly exist, and study even at a secondary level must usually be based on specialized monographs and articles. Often, however, even these are sparse, and some recourse to original sources, printed or manuscript, must be had. All this seems to support the view that local history is more of a postgraduate study than one that the undergraduate, let alone the school pupil, can tackle. We must be careful, however, not to exaggerate the force of this argument when considering local history in school. All history at its highest levels requires ripe scholarship, yet because such maturity can be obtained only by long study over the years there is all the more reason why it should be started early. Only a tiny minority of the population goes on to read history at the post-school level, and it would be unthinkable to deny the vast majority of citizens some introduction to history in school. Furthermore teachers in adult education have developed techniques whereby knowledge of general history is gained concurrently with local history. There is no reason why the same practice should not be applied to the study of local history in school.

More serious objections, however, have been levelled against the use of local history in the classroom in anything but a purely ancillary capacity. W. H. Burston has argued that the unit of study in the school history syllabus should be of such a size that an explanation of events is largely possible within the confines of the unit chosen. The history of England, at least from 1485, is a feasible unit, but the events in a locality cannot be explained largely by a study of the locality itself.[1] While this argument contains some obvious truths there are nevertheless some clear objections to it. Most obviously, national history itself often cannot be explained without reference to extra-national history, yet one would not deny that national history is a proper area of study in school. Burston's views derive from an over-riding belief that the core of history is political history and that other branches of history are examples of what he terms 'aspect history'.

Public affairs, like private life, are not, however, divided into water-tight compartments as 'political', 'economic', 'social' 'religious' and so on. One suspects that the creed of the paramount importance of political history is a legacy of the interests of the Victorians, influenced by the continued dominance in university history syllabuses of this kind of history, and the unfortunate fact that professional historians have permitted their subject to become fragmented in special university departments and faculties, with political history being the prime concern of the 'history' departments. Yet it could be argued that political history is as much 'aspect history' as is economic, and few would maintain that political events in the past have always been more important than economic ones, if indeed political, social and economic factors are anyway extricable one from the other.

If we admit that economic and social aspects of the lives of communities are as equally worthy of study as political ones, then the claim for some attention to be given to the study of local history is strengthened. For in the fields of economic and social history, particularly when we are dealing with periods before the present century, local variations were more considerable than they were in political affairs. National generalizations in these areas are often difficult, and even at times impossible or meaningless. The history of the locality must be taken into account if pupils are to understand what life in the past was like. This is not to argue that teaching about the locality is more important than teaching about national history but to emphasize that both have a claim for inclusion in the history syllabus.

Antiquarianism and parochialism

Local history must not, however, be included without serious thought, for there are dangers and limitations which if ignored may result in more harm than good. First, the teacher as much as the student generally must beware of antiquarianism. Professor Hoskins's warning that local history as purveyed by antiquarians is not history at all, and that real local historians must be concerned with problems, is relevant to teaching local history in school. Not all knowledge is worthwhile knowledge, and it is the teacher's duty to structure and to lead. To put the authority of his knowledge at the pupils' disposal through guidance is not to be 'authoritarian' in a pejorative sense. Both in the selection of local topics for study and in the choice of the materials and tasks involved the teacher must be aware of their place in the general objectives of his syllabus. Such objectives will include not only the understanding of the national and local history of a certain period or a certain theme and their interrelationship but also the skills and interests they are intended to develop. The merely quaint, the merely old, the merely attractive must not long deflect the class or teacher from basic aims. Open-ended unstructured involvement with the locality and its history is not an effective learning technique and is not justified even with younger children. In using local history the subject matter must be relevant to the whole course and the local material must be in itself worthwhile.

The worst kind of 'local history' one observes being conducted in schools is as part of a 'local study' where the scraps of random history involved do not fit into any structure of knowledge the child already possesses, are not a reasoned part of any new body of knowledge, and are therefore significant at best only to the teacher. The observation of a Roundhead cannonball in the wall of the parish church is largely meaningless unless seen in light of some knowledge of the Civil War generally, or as a lead into or part of a study of the war locally or nationally. Local history 'trails', where random observations or 'discoveries' are made on local canals, factories and so on, unless placed in the context of local and national industry and communications in a specific period, are likely to be of minimal value. They may well help to produce embryonic antiquarians rather than adults with some conception of history as a study of change and of the intricacies and interactions of human endeavour.

The teacher must always be aware of the reason for the study of any particular topic, and equally the reason for any exercise or activity undertaken as part of that study, and be able to justify them. He will then reject certain activities which are superficially enjoyable and vaguely related to history, or he will inject some purpose by building on them. Rubbings of brass effigies or tombstones, for example, are interesting to children and may have peripheral value for the development of artistic skills—but their value for history must be doubted if the activity ends there, and is not part of or does not lead into a general study of such topics as the lives of the persons commemorated, the status of those wealthy enough to be buried in a privileged way inside the church, the place of the parish church in the life of the community, the significance of child mortality, and so on. Again the common exercise of using baptismal registers to compare the popularity of children's christian names today with those common, say, in the seventeenth century may give practice in simple arithmetic but has no value for their understanding of the past or the present unless it is the basis of deeper questions, perhaps in this case to bring out the influence of puritanism. Much the same criticism could be made of the study of heraldry in school if it exists only at the level of art work or as an introduction to unrelated specialist knowledge. Always, then, the teacher must ask, Why am I doing this? What will the children learn from it? Could the time be more fruitfully spent? Later chapters in this book seek to help him in the necessary process of selecting appropriate materials for children's study of relevant aspects of local history.

Another danger the teacher must avoid is that of inculcating through local history a narrow inward-looking parochialism. The adult historian with a sound general knowledge of history is able to spend much time on the minutiæ of local history without getting its significance out of proportion. Children do not have this background, so that their local studies must always go hand in hand with learning about general history. Environmental studies as practised at their worst in British schools have been found to be intellectually restrictive,[2] and the same can be said of local history of the parish-pump type. The pupil should not leave school either knowing nothing about the history of anywhere but his own region (for if he does he will not even know anything of value about that) or having a distorted view of the significance of his own locality in the past. The likelihood of 'parochial distortion' is, however, an argument not against the teaching of local history but against the teaching of local history badly. As W. E. Tate has put it, 'local history . . . may well begin with the parish pump—it should never end there'.

A connected danger lies in misplaced enthusiasm—the belief that what interests the teacher will or should necessarily interest the child. Of course an adult's enthusiasm is infectious and can legitimately be tapped in the classroom, but it must not be allowed to distort the general education of his pupils. Some history teachers have turned to local history because they have become bored teaching the same lessons year after year. Their new-found interest may initially stimulate freshness of approach and interest on the part of the children, even when the topics, methods and material are in some ways inappropriate to the pupils' needs. But the teacher must realize, that not only is the general history, so well trodden to him, new to the children, and too important often to deny them, but that the local history will also become to him well trodden. The adoption of local history is not a permanent answer to boredom and dullness. Such a solution is more likely to come from the fusion of his new interest with his old topics, and from the opportunity the materials of local history provide for ringing the changes and introducing a degree of novelty.

Activity, discovery and 'research'

A further pitfall is the conscription of local history to serve too un-critically adopted methodological approaches: in particular the overemphasis of 'activity' and 'discovery' methods. It is true that 'activity' methods, provided the activity has a purpose, have their value. But the acceleration of learning can hardly take place without the development of literary skills. The reaction against the over-bookish didacticism of the past is in danger of going too far. Local history, perhaps more than other aspects of history has a valuable practical side to it, but this advantage must not be abused. By itself, without any intellectual underpinning, the value of practical work is limited, and the fact that there are few local history books written specifically for children should not be made an excuse for over-emphasizing it. Visits, fieldwork, modelling, and the like should be used in conjunction with and to foster literary and verbal work. The use of reference books and source material, the compilation of lists, graphs, descriptive accounts, the writing of stories, discussions and the teacher's oral explanation are essential to a rounded educational approach. There is, moreover, always the need to relate local aspects of a topic to national developments, and for these textbooks and other books appropriate to the ages and abilities of the pupils will be available. There is no excuse for allowing the study of local history to contribute to anti-intellectualism. If used properly it can give as great an opportunity for intellectual work as most traditional school subjects; and it can offer different types of work suitable for children from the junior school onwards. In both junior and secondary schools, for example, it lends itself to the use of project work, in-cluding projects with mixed ability classes, since any single topic offers considerable diversity of content and of associated tasks. Because this is so, however, care must be taken that children of lower ability are not continually allowed to apply themselves to tasks requiring little thought and little development of literary skills, with the more academic aspects monopolized by the brighter pupils. Likewise average and above-average children should not be permitted to spend too much time on practical work.

The 'discovery' method in education, with its impressive pedigree from Rousseau onwards, has long had considerable influence in

junior schools, and its alleged success there has resulted in its continuing extension to secondary-school work. One of the besetting sins
of modern educationists is, however, the belief that merit in one
approach necessarily excludes any value in others, and that methods
which suit some subjects must needs suit all. Overemphasis of the
part played by 'discovery' and 'learning by experience' in the cognitive process, especially when such terms are interpreted to suggest
that the teacher has or ought to play little part in the development of
the child, has led to unwarranted scorn being poured on more
traditional methods, in particular that of verbal exposition. While we
must reject any return to the 'rote learning' pedagogy of the past we
must also accept that 'the notion that a child must follow through all
the stages of human development to discover what his predecessors
have already found out is ridiculous'.[3] This means that the teacher's
role is not that of the filler of empty vessels with predigested knowledge, but rather that of the knowledgeable guide pointing the way and
explaining the difficulties. And as with the method, so with content.
Not all knowledge is worth acquiring; some aspects of knowledge
relate logically to others, some do not. In all learning the teacher must
play a part; it may be to structure the learning environment so that
certain 'discoveries' are made; or to suggest reading certain books or
undertaking certain tasks in a particular sequence; or to lecture and
to present—for 'talk and chalk' remains an invaluable teaching
method so long as it is not used exclusively. All this is most relevant
to the humanities generally, and to history in particular, for the bulk
of knowledge of the past cannot be learnt by direct or simulated
experience. In particular much may be 'discovered' from books. This
is not to suggest, however, that there are not practical difficulties here.
For the average child and for those of lower ability there is a limited
number of suitable reference books, and many such children are not
capable of understanding much of the vocabulary traditionally used
by historians and teachers.[4] But this really again reinforces the
argument against unfettered 'freedom' for the child to find out for
himself,[5] and much recent thought and research indicates that the
claims for a dominant role in education for discovery methods are no
more justified on psychological than on philosophical grounds.[6]

Consequently, when stressing the opportunities local history offers
for the use by children of original source materials (both in the form
of documents and of physical remains), we must not give credence to
the view that here is a way of adopting wholesale, to the exclusion of all
else, the heuristic process in the learning of history. Much misguided

enthusiasm has gone to spread the view that documents, and especially the documents of local history, can be used to introduce historical 'research' into schools—'research' here being often a pseudonym for 'discovery'. Genuine research (the attempt to discover by investigation new facts on which to base new theories, or to reconsider accepted judgements with a view to revising them) can be undertaken only by those who are well versed in the general field being investigated and trained in the techniques required for investigation. If, however, the background has already been explained by the teacher and studied by the pupil, and the child is then required to perceive how various aspects of the subject are illustrated from a document or other source, this is quite legitimate. It is a form of guided investigation ('discovery', if you like) which is really a variant of explanatory teaching and which is so much more effective than the popular 'personal discovery from scratch' methods. This is not, however, research in the proper sense and it would be best not to term it so. The pupil is not equipped, without guidance, to ask of the document significant questions, or to use it in the way a mature student can. It would do the child an injustice to allow him to believe that he had discovered something significantly new or put a fresh interpretation upon an historical problem. He may well, however, have found out something he himself did not know before, or at least acquired greater insight into what he had already been told or read, and in some cases will remember it better than merely reading a generalized sentence or two in a textbook. But he must not be led to think that real historians make important deductions from isolated records, for that would give no insight at all into how historians work.

It has been claimed that local history, with its variety of readily available original sources, can be used to contrive ' "closed research situations" . . . in which pupils can be given a chance to attempt some of the diverse demands of the study of the past by following the processes used by professional historians—initial reading, posing of questions, collection of evidence, and drawing of conclusions'.[7] In fact these processes—reading, collection, questions, analysis, conclusions—are common to the essay or project work of the secondary pupil and the undergraduate and to the textbook writer, and are not unique to the original researcher. All that is being said is that the use of local sources may promote skill in those processes traditionally fostered by the good history teacher—of course an acceptable and an added recommendation for such use. A teacher may, for example, set a class to collect from census enumerators' books statistics which

have not been prepared before, and from these may be drawn conclusions about, say, the percentage of persons in a particular street
in a particular town in 1851 who had been born in Ireland. The
mechanics of compiling such statistics, though involving the techniques of the adult researcher, do not comprise the totality of research; nor does the limited conclusion come into this category, for
the significance of a conclusion is to be judged only in the context of
deep specialized knowledge. Nevertheless the child here has experienced something akin to adult research, and occasional exercises
of this kind may be useful. They are, however, extremely time-
consuming, and it is often doubtful whether the returns are worth
the effort, even with older secondary-school children.

The task of the history teacher, in junior and secondary schools,
is not only to stimulate learning by personal enquiry but also to foster
it by explanation and instruction. This is perhaps the most important
reason for making use of original sources in teaching local history.
In particular, as later chapters will seek to demonstrate, local sources
provide an almost limitless fund of examples to illustrate the local
and general history being taught. They can be used, too, as stimulus
material to introduce the study of new topics. Their use for comprehension purposes—as to deduce from a factory commission
report the various evils of child labour in nineteenth-century cotton
districts—is also a legitimate one, though it can become tedious if
overemployed. 'Nose to the work card' week after week, even when
the work card includes documentary material, may tend to the neglect
of the essentials of good history teaching, which include verbal
exposition and explanation, and the oral interaction between class and
teacher that derives from discussion. The pupil will get more out of
the use of documents, which it is the intent of this book to promote,
if they are used within a varied teaching structure where the guiding
and explanatory role of the teacher is well developed.

Factors affecting the use of local history

Local history, essentially part of general history, is most fruitfully
used within a history syllabus, but it can be employed to considerable
advantage in various forms of integrated studies. In particular, in
'local studies' and 'environmental studies', which are primarily
concerned with the present and restricted topographically and
chronologically, it can provide the dimension of time and, moreover,
bring pupils into contact with a range of new areas of knowledge.
Local history can also enrich such interdisciplinary courses as 'social

studies' and 'humanities'. But, however local history is used, teachers will need to take into account such practical matters as the periods being studied, the ages, abilities and social backgrounds of their pupils, and the physical situation of their school.

When periods before the sixteenth or seventeenth centuries are being taught local history is often best used in an illustrative way, though later chapters will show that there are some topics in those periods for which suitable sources and sufficient information are available for study at a purely local level. For the early modern period, and more particularly for the eighteenth and nineteenth centuries, however, records concerned with many aspects of local history which are understandable and attractive to children of different ages will be varied and plentiful. There will be much pictorial, and later photographic, material and maps, and literary sources will be commoner and easier to comprehend, while for the nineteenth and early twentieth centuries inexpensive physical objects will be common. For these most recent centuries, then, there will be scope for the study of local history in its own right, in a limited way with younger children and more extensively with older children capable of more advanced and prolonged study. With older secondary-school children of average intelligence and above, however, the teaching of local history in its own right may be limited by the requirements of public examination syllabuses. In this case the tendency will naturally be to use local history primarily to illustrate general history, whatever the period being studied.

In choosing topics for study for local history in its own right the teacher will be guided by a number of factors. He will need to select aspects, documents, tasks and so on which are commensurate with the time available. In integrated studies he will need to stress those aspects which can best contribute to such work—as, for example, the study of topography, housing, social structure, and so on. For mixed-ability classes of any age he will need to select topics and materials which lend themselves to diverse group and project work including practical activities.

The social background of pupils may also need to be taken into account, especially where predominantly neighbourhood schools are concerned. In certain types of district, for example, homes will have few resources (such as books) to be tapped; the estate children's knowledge of their own locality is often very restricted, and in poorer areas opportunities for visiting near-by sites and buildings with parents may be limited. Unfortunately these children are often the very ones less likely to be provided with funds from home to take part in school expeditions designed to make good their general unawareness of the neighbourhood. There is need for Heads and history teachers to press for assistance here—and to emphasize that fieldwork is an integral part of any syllabus which includes local history.

The part of the country in which the school is situated will also affect the sort of local history taught. Not all aspects of national history can be illustrated from the history of any particular locality. In some places there will be Roman remains, while other schools will have no traces of the Roman occupation near them. In urban areas illustration of recent agricultural history may be difficult, and conversely teachers in certain rural districts will not be able to provide examples of industrial development. Maritime history can clearly feature in the local history only of certain places; some aspects of political history—the Civil War, Chartism and so on—will be easier to illustrate from the history of some places than of others. Even where different parts of the country shared in the same movement the emphasis may differ—cotton will feature largely in the study of the industrial revolution in Lancashire, coal and iron in Wales. The availability of suitable source materials will also affect the topics the teacher can utilize. Factors involved here will be not only the actual history of the region but the survival of records, the proximity to record offices and libraries, and the extent to which these have adapted themselves to the needs of history teachers.

There is the question, too, of what the teacher is to consider as 'local' in planning his syllabus. Should local history be that of the immediate neighbourhood of the school, or of the town in which it is situated, or should it cover a larger area—perhaps a county or even a region? One cannot be dogmatic: what is 'local' as far as school history is concerned will vary from area to area, from school to school, from age group to age group. It will also vary according to the topic being studied. Clearly what is in the first instance 'local' to the informed adult is not necessarily 'local' to the pupil. To children, particularly young children, living in one London borough the contiguous borough may be as remote as Manchester or Dundee. On the other hand children from Leeds may be more familiar with Scarborough Castle than the nearer York Minster, or even than parts of Leeds, for the seaside resort is part of their environment—extended by the summer day trip.

This does not mean, however, that local history in school must be restricted territorially to the area the pupils are familiar with. If that were so children resident in recently built council estates or modern suburbs could be offered comparatively little local history. It is part of the job of the teacher of local history to build up knowledge of an extended locality, so that, while with juniors much work will be concentrated in areas not too distant from the school, over a period of time a child should become aware of the relationship of his village and others to the neighbouring town, of his suburb and others to the town centre, of the relation of the town to near-by towns, of the place of the town in the region, and so on. This is why fieldwork of various kinds and much topographical and map work should be an integral part of the local history taught. In these days of easier communications the locality that can be experienced by the child is larger than was once the case.

In practice the teacher will have also to take larger topographical areas for the study of some topics than of others, depending once more on the situation of the school. For certain periods, particularly the Middle Ages and before, the area may have to be quite large. For Liverpool children Chester may be the obvious place to use for the study of Roman and medieval life, and since the history of the two ports was later so interconnected this would certainly not distort the theme 'local'. Conversely, for Chester children Manchester, Liverpool and Warrington may be sufficiently 'local' to use in studying the industrial revolution. Bradford has no monastic remains, but several are within easy travelling distance.

It is unlikely that suitable source material for every topic will be available for the immediate locality. Manorial court rolls or poor-law records, for example, may exist for a neighbouring village or town rather than one's own, the only enclosure map may be for a parish twenty miles away. In such cases these records will have to be used, and this will have the advantage of extending the child's knowledge of his region. Certain topics by their nature cannot in any case be studied in too parochial a way. Where the region is more significant than the town this must be taken into account. So in treating the history of communications, of trade and industry, and perhaps of agriculture, study of a larger area than the village or town will often be both necessary and appropriate.

It must be remembered, too, that while such units as the parish and the hundred had some meaning in the past they are not necessarily proper units for local study today. In large towns children, and adults too, are often unaware what parish they reside in, and parochial boundaries have long ceased to have much significance. Likewise in large concentrations where town merges with town even borough boundaries are not of overriding significance in the study of many aspects of social and economic local history.

Some thought, then, will need to be given to ways of introducing local history into the syllabus. If it is to be used solely to illustrate general history it will not be too difficult to provide local examples at appropriate places or in certain cases to devote time to local events of national significance—like Peterloo in Manchester, Marston Moor in York. Where purely local history is to be given special attention, then more planning is required.

The suggestion that 'for the most part the local material would be put over by means of "brief oral intrusions" with occasional short research exercises'[8] is to my mind too unambitious, and later chapters will give plenty of suggestions for much more detailed and pupil-centred work than this, and work which will require a much less casual connection with the history syllabus as a whole. There are several possible ways of achieving this. Some teachers favour the setting aside of a whole term or even a year, and devoting all history lessons entirely to local history. Usually this occurs in the last year of the junior school, or in the secondary school in the years before public examination work begins.[9] Some merit attaches to this procedure, for pupils are made clearly aware that their area has a history of its own, is not identical with that of other areas, and is of sufficient significance for time to be devoted exclusively to it. If this block approach is to be followed logical organization is needed, and though no single method can be recommended some suggestions as to procedure may be given. Several weeks, or even a whole term, might, for example, be devoted to a survey of the region from the point of view of physical features, communications, patterns of settlement and natural resources. This would involve visits to other towns in the region and to physically distinctive geographical areas within it, so that the region becomes tangibly 'local' to the pupils. In subsequent weeks, or a second term, group work might be undertaken, with projects on different aspects of the local past—topically or chronologically based, as, for example, industrial activity, local government, the Roman period, and the Middle Ages. For each group the teacher will need to provide a general outline, a list of reference works, and appropriate reproductions of maps, pictures and records. In some cases work cards may be a suitable means to further the work. Further weeks, or a third term, could well be devoted to consolidation, such as presentation of the work in booklets, exhibitions of one sort or another, dramatic exercises, and if possible children should be involved in work requiring the examination of the findings of groups other than their own. In addition the teacher would do well to provide explanatory and discussion lessons at the outset and at intervals throughout the course, to provide a sufficient framework of knowledge for the project work to be meaningful to the participants.

Such a method of treating local history does have disadvantages. If it is undertaken at the junior or early secondary stage the pupil is unlikely to have sufficient knowledge of general history to appreciate the significance of local developments. Moreover when history as a whole is given so few periods in the timetable the devotion of such a large proportion to local history is likely to detract from the proper learning of general history. With older children, however, concentrated courses on purely local history are more profitable. There are several ways of doing this. At fifth-form level there may be a place for it as a post-examination exercise, sufficiently novel, and involving fieldwork and visits, for it to be fresh and interesting. But it can also be incorporated in the public examination syllabus. This may be easiest with the CSE examination, which can embrace not only written examination papers but the presentation of individual course work as a personal topic.[10] Most GCE boards, however, are willing to consider setting at O level papers which will include questions or sections on the local history of the school's area, provided a syllabus is agreed between school and board. If such a course is decided on it would, however, seem desirable that it should not comprise the whole of the examination syllabus, and that it should not range in time over too extended a period, but be related to the period of general history being studied. It seems likely that the personal topic will find an increasing place in GCE syllabuses, too, and clearly local topics would be very suitable. The Schools Council project on history for the thirteen-to-sixteen age group has suggested local history as a suitable area for the examination syllabus for the last two years before the school-leaving age. At GCE A level the advantage of using local examples is already accepted, and preparation for it can profitably include the use of original material in local record offices.[11] Those pupils studying subjects at A level other than history may also find that local history assists in certain aspects of their own specialist subjects—geography, economics, sociology. This will be especially so when the local history studied stresses social and economic aspects, fieldwork and industrial and traditional archaeology. A short course on local history may also be popular as part of the non-examination part of the sixth-form curriculum. The adolescent of this age will often be more mature, have greater background knowledge, and be able to undertake more advanced work, theoretical and practical, than younger pupils.

At most stages in a child's school career, however, concentrated courses on local history are less appropriate in teaching the subject in its own right than are other methods. Where a 'lines of development' type of history syllabus is in use detailed consideration of local aspects of each appropriate topic can be included as a matter of course. Thus in industrial Lancashire and the Midlands one might expect time to be spent on local canal development, in the West Country local aspects of agricultural history might be stressed. And there would be scope, where project work was undertaken, for some groups to devote themselves entirely to local aspects of the theme being followed. Most secondary schools, however, favour a chronologically arranged history syllabus where depth is provided by the 'patch' method of giving certain topics, periods or events much more detailed treatment than others, and, of course, the 'patch' approach is also appropriate to junior-school children. In such cases local history in its own right is most suitably introduced as a series of 'patches'. Thus, for example, the study of Victorian England by Lincolnshire pupils can include a patch on nineteenth-century Lincoln stressing both its similarities with the country generally and its differences. In this way the logical development of the locality is gradually absorbed, and fitted into the context of national history, without local history being allowed to dominate the syllabus in any particular term or year.

In environmental and social studies, both in junior and in secondary schools, the scope for the introduction of local history will be determined by the type of syllabus, and variations of syllabuses are too many for any detailed advice to be given here.[12] In junior schools the 'then and now' approach is often favoured, where the present is contrasted with the comparatively recent past, including the Victorian period. This at least creates an awareness of development and change as well as continuity in a local community, and of the existence of history in the world about us, and so is not without value for younger children. Where integrated studies are used in the secondary school, and especially where history has been absorbed by these rather than continuing alongside, the history specialist has a responsibility to inject, at least for children of average ability and above, a more sophisticated approach.[13] For such pupils something of what the

study of history as a distinct discipline has to offer should be pre-
served. Since history is concerned with change and continuity, and
with the complexities of the relationship of people and events, the
historian should attempt to instil into pupils following such courses
awareness of the time factor—that there were many 'thens', that not
all about them can necessarily be related to our 'now', and that to see
the past only as a backward extension of the present is superficial. If
pupils following integrated courses can be made aware of these
aspects of history, local and national, something worthwhile will have
been achieved. With below-average secondary pupils, this may
unfortunately be too ambitious, and the history specialist must then
be content, *faute de mieux*, to contribute in a humbler way. This may
especially be necessary with less able 'school leavers', with whom
integrated syllabuses devoted to a direct study of the environment
may bear more fruit than the traditional 'subject' and 'lesson' approach.
In such schemes the background of local history will have a place.
Often work will take the form of local surveys, and teachers involved
will find information in later chapters, especially Chapter 8, of rele-
vance to them here. They may, too, profitably seek to show the
chronological relationship between the local history studied as a
background to different topics. The child has little difficulty in per-
ceiving the connections between aspects of contemporary life (as
housing, population, industry, communications) studied sequentially.
It is more difficult to relate historical information about these topics—
and help is needed to understand that the penny-farthing and the
spinning jenny, both 'history', were not contemporaneous. For all
pupils local history can also be used as an antidote to the generalizations that the social science basis of many social studies courses tends
to stress. It can be shown, for example, that different places had
different experiences, that conditions were not identical everywhere
at the same time.

For notes to this chapter see pp. 164–5.

3 Preparing to teach local history

The teacher of local history must be concerned both with the content and the methodology of his subject: the actual history of his region and the available sources, as well as the techniques used by local historians. Yet, despite the growth of local history in schools, comparatively few teachers are adequately equipped to teach it. University undergraduate courses rarely include local history, and though specialist history students in colleges of education give it more attention, problems of time limit the extent to which it can be pursued, as is the case in university education departments. Moreover students go to teach in areas different from those they studied in, and much local history, particularly in junior and middle schools, is taught, as history or in integrated studies, by those who have not specialized in the subject at college.

Skilled teaching of local history is, however, hampered less by the lack of student study of the subject than—especially at secondary-school level—by unfamiliarity with general social and economic history, for much local history is essentially economic and social. The basic diet for history undergraduates, and to a lesser extent for college students, is political history. Consequently the teaching of social and economic history before the sixth form is often weaker than the treatment of political history—despite the increasing emphasis in schools on these aspects of history. Those who teach them thus tend too often to teach in an antiquarian way, and to provide simplistic and outdated content, taking their teaching materials from old and over-simplified textbooks, and failing to draw on detailed advanced works because unaware of their existence. Teaching of sound local history on such a basis is impossible.

It is probably unwise to look for radical changes in university and college curricula for improvement in the situation. One can sympathize with the complaints that history degrees and teaching qualifications are obtainable without the student ever having examined a single primary source of evidence, and without any knowledge of archaeology, palaeography, sociology, anthropology or demography. Yet sober reflection will suggest that such views, however well intended, are misguided. Many important historical works are based not on primary sources of evidence at first hand, but on reassessment of the findings and opinions of other historians; and many an acknowledgedly great modern historian would be unable to read a word of the very medieval charter that an able extra-mural student could transcribe and translate. History undergraduates, furthermore, often use published primary sources, particularly in their special options, and a growing number follow courses in sociology, archaeology and other ancillary subjects. Some, perhaps too few, have an opportunity to learn such subjects as palaeography and historical demography. That these activities are usually optional and not compulsory is, however, defensible. History embraces and is connected with many specialisms. It is not necessary to be familiar with all to be a good historian; what is essential is to study what one does in some depth. To some specialist historical studies an acquaintance with the methods and nature of anthropology, sociology and social psychology may have some value; to others medieval Latin, archaeology or Renaissance art may be more relevant. The imposition of all or a wide variety of those specialist studies on every undergraduate or college student could lead only to the superficiality and uniformity British universities and colleges have been wise to eschew.

Moreover it would be undesirable for university courses to be influenced by the needs of the school curriculum, for the university teacher has wider responsibilities. What may be pleaded for here, however, not merely in the interests of school teaching but on behalf of Clio herself, is a lessening of the fragmentation of historical studies in the universities and a greater realization that political history is as much a facet, or aspect, of history as are economic history and social history, and no more. It can no longer claim to be the core of history. We may hope, too, that more local history special topics and options may emerge in those university departments devoted to the different aspects of history. And the student intent on a teaching career might well consider the advantage of choosing such options.

A little can be done to introduce students to local history in their postgraduate teaching certificate course, but if there is time to supplement undergraduate studies it may lie more in providing some introduction to medieval history generally and to general social and economic history for those students whose degree work did not adequately cover those areas.

In colleges of education the case for making the history syllabus conform more to the needs of the school curriculum is stronger and the scope for local history consequently greater. Since the training course lasts for three or four years, with intermittent long vacations, there may be a little more opportunity for specialization in local history and its methodology. College tutors have noted, however, that where their students do work with archives as part of their special studies they probably have less academic background than graduates to interpret the material they wish to use in class. Thus here again a firm grounding in national political, economic and social history is to be preferred to premature specialization in local aspects. It must be recognized, too, that even where a student does leave college or university with some acquaintance with the sources and methods of local history, and having studied the history of a particular region, his knowledge will be limited.

So while we may not fully agree with the view that local history is, as far as the adult student is concerned, primarily a postgraduate pursuit, the future of sound local history in schools is likely to lie in the further education or self-education of those serving teachers who already have a good academic grounding in national history. Here higher education establishments can provide an important service by offering part- or full-time courses in sources and techniques in the local history of their districts, and in teaching local history. There is particular scope here for the provision of courses for teachers in their induction year and for older teachers on secondment. In addition to attendance at taught courses personal work by teachers, perhaps for a higher degree, on an aspect of local history can be invaluable. The pursuit of theses topics, apparently narrow in scope, will be found to lead to a surprisingly wide-ranging knowledge of the locality in the past and into the nature and techniques of local history generally.

Local authorities can help directly by providing, in teachers' centres and the like, facilities for teachers to meet and discuss and to hear talks from outside experts. They can encourage and assist the establishment of resources centres and co-operate with other local government departments, especially archive departments, and libraries.

The teacher's preliminary reading

With or without the help of formal instruction the individual teacher will need to do much work before being able to cope effectively with teaching local history. Some will always teach in areas where they have some knowledge of the local past. Many, however, will at some time or other teach in places where they do not possess such a back-ground. Given that he has a good up-to-date knowledge of national history, the teacher intending to use local history in class will first need to acquire a sound understanding of the history of his region in the national context. This will not result from a few hours by the fireside with a book or two. When the young teacher has settled down and feels able to cope with the normal school curriculum he should begin to prepare himself in a disciplined way to introduce local history into his syllabus.

His initial task will be to familiarize himself with the study of local history generally and the sort of topics and questions which local historians consider significant. These embrace, for example, the history at various periods of local institutions, of local government, of politics and of religion, educational, agricultural, industrial and commercial aspects of local life, as well as demography and social structure, social conditions, poor relief, topography, architecture and similar topics. There are a number of general works (see p. 163) which will provide a sound introduction, and having done preliminary reading of this sort the teacher must then seek to master in some depth the general history of the district in which he lives in the regional setting. This task should not be pursued haphazardly by unsystematic dipping into such books as may be available by chance. Shelves of local libraries groan with bad and indifferent books on local history, and the advice of some local amateur 'experts' should be regarded with suspicion. The best professional guidance will probably be that of the reference librarian in charge of the local collection, the local archivist, or the full-time WEA or university extra-mural tutor in local history. Some older town and county histories are of outstanding and prevailing value, but it is necessary to seek advice on which these are. To begin with it would probably be wise to seek out the most recent works on the local history of the district written by professional historians, such as (to give one example out of many) A. D. Dyer's *The City of Worcester in the Sixteenth Century* (1973). The 'Making of the English Landscape' county series (Hodder & Stoughton) provides up-to-date texts and bibliographies and will often prove a good introduction to further reading. For some counties series of introductory histories exist, such as those published by the Cheshire Community Council and by the History of Lincolnshire Committee.[1]

For many parts of the country the volumes of the *Victoria County History* will provide a good starting place, especially if they have been published fairly recently. The *V.C.H.* plans to provide a series of volumes for each English county, comprising 'general' volumes and 'topographical' volumes, and over 130 volumes have already been published. The 'general' volumes cover for the whole county such aspects as prehistory, ecclesiastical history including monasteries, political history, agriculture, economic and social history, and grammar schools. Very important for the teacher is the inclusion in these general volumes for many counties of a translation of the county section of Domesday with index and commentary. The 'topographical' volumes deal in detail with the history of each individual town or parish under such aspects as manors, churches, charities, Roman Catholicism, Nonconformity, schools, local government and economic history, and also devote a great deal of attention to topography. Nevertheless a great deal of factual information is provided, and some large towns like Birmingham, Coventry, York and Hull receive treatment more akin to that of the general volumes. A general guide to the contents of the *V.C.H.* has been published,[2] and local libraries are likely to have all volumes pertaining to their county.

At this stage the teacher would be wise to make himself familiar with good recent monographs on the history of industries or other enterprises important in his particular region. Not only clearly regional studies such as Herbert Heaton, *Yorkshire Woollen and Worsted Industries* (Oxford, 1920) and W. H. Court, *The Rise of the Midland Industries* (1938), but also more general monographs like J. U. Nef, *The Rise of the British Coal Industry* (1932) and P. J. Bowden, *The Wool Trade in Tudor and Stuart England* (1962).

Similarly when the region was significantly affected by or concerned in a particular event or movement in national history up-to-date knowledge of the general history of that topic will be needed. So for many northern and midland towns a good recent history of the industrial revolution (not books produced for schools), and for certain rural areas a similar study of agricultural history will be essential.[3]

Having made himself familiar with the general history of the region and its place in the national context, the teacher's next task is to compile a list of important events and topics distinguishing which were peculiarly local and which were shared in common with other localities. Without the basic knowledge both of local history and its techniques, and of the history of his region, it is profitless to go on to the next stage, and the over-zealous should beware of proceeding without these foundations. If they are well laid, however, the teacher may now survey the local sources, printed and manuscript, which are available to illustrate and elaborate the main themes and events, local and national, of the periods he wishes to teach. In doing so it will be necessary to choose those items which are most likely to be attractive and comprehensible to pupils of varying age groups, and which may be suitable for the sort of classwork described elsewhere in this volume.

Surveying the sources

Certain kinds of primary source materials are particularly relevant to the teaching of local history. They fall mainly into three groups: published records; unpublished records; and physical sources, such as sites and buildings. There is a natural tendency for the uninformed to be impatient to make use of unpublished materials, particularly manuscripts. Such an urge must be kept in check, for a great mass of important material is readily available in print and can give quicker and often more substantial returns than an undisciplined wallowing in manuscript collections. Many printed records are, moreover, more suitable for teaching purposes. First, there are those primary sources which were themselves printed and published, and which, from the nineteenth century, may well form the bulk of useful materials. To these I will return soon. Then most counties or groups of counties and some towns possess local record societies which publish important local records in full or abbreviated form. These are easier to read than the originals and usually accompanied by useful notes and commentaries. Sometimes early records are published in the original Latin, but many appear in translation and then have an added value for most teachers. Local reference libraries will certainly have sets of the publications of these societies, many of which began their work in the nineteenth century and have a large number of published volumes to their credit. If indexes or catalogues are not available E. L. C. Mullins, *Texts and Calendars* (Royal Hist. Soc., 1958) provides a useful guide to the contents of the publications of many societies. Mullins not only lists individual volumes but provides a subject index so that the reader may quickly find out whether, for example, his local society has reproduced any parish register, any local manorial court roll, any farmer's notebooks, and so on.

Other record societies exist which do not confine themselves to the records concerning any particular area, and the searcher may sometimes find that vital local records have been reproduced in such a series. The Early English Text Society, for example, has published the extensive records of the Coventry leet court, which provide a rich storehouse of information on life in that town. Other such societies include the Selden Society and the Camden Society.

Some national records which contain much on various localities have been published in full or calendared (i.e. abridged) form by government agencies, and may be found in larger reference libraries. The Record Commission has, for example, published the Domesday Book and some of the Hundred Rolls. The Public Record Office has produced calendars of certain collections, of which the teacher will find most useful the *Calendar of State Papers, Domestic* and the *Acts of the Privy Council*. Some collections of local records, including those of a number of towns, are to be found in the publications of the Royal Commission on Historical Manuscripts (HMC), also to be found in large libraries.[4] A whole volume, for example, is devoted to the records of the city of Exeter.

Some records, particularly for the Middle Ages, have been published by record societies, and other bodies, in the original Latin. In this case where the teacher cannot read medieval Latin he can nevertheless probably identify volumes or sections which pertain to his locality, and he should seek the aid of a better equipped colleague, or other expert—perhaps via the local history society—to obtain relevant translations. Often only a limited knowledge of Latin is needed to make sense of such records as charters, court rolls and other common records.

Of primary sources which were themselves published the most important are undoubtedly parliamentary papers, local newspapers, local directories and Ordnance Survey maps. Parliamentary papers, sometimes called 'Blue Books', embrace the reports of parliamentary committees and Royal Commissions, and the reports of government inspectors of various kinds (as mines inspectors, factory inspectors, school inspectors, etc) and of boards (like the Poor Law Board), Ministries and other government departments, as well as 'accounts and papers. These include information on a multitude of topics, including agriculture, trade and industry, labour, transport, poor law, health, housing, town planning, education, police and so on. The reports and more particularly the appendixes of evidence frequently contain a great deal of information on different localities. The nature of a few, such as the factory inspectors' reports, will be well known to teachers, because they are frequently quoted in textbooks, but there are many more which can bring life to history in the classroom. Until recently they have been difficult for teachers to use

because few libraries had many accessible volumes. Now photographic reproductions are available as well as microcard editions and
an increasing number of town and city libraries have bought them.
Those that have not should be encouraged by teachers, local education authorities and others interested in local history to do so, and
also to make accessible the original volumes which so often reside in
surprisingly large numbers in mouldering oblivion in inaccessible
store rooms. It is difficult to exaggerate the value of parliamentary
papers for teaching purposes, and teachers should, therefore, familiarize themselves with official and other indexes to which librarians
will be able to refer them. A useful short selection is provided in W.
R. Powell's *Local History from Blue Books* (Hist. Assoc., 1969),
which lists under topic headings those parliamentary papers most
useful for local historians.

Local libraries, at least in the larger towns, usually possess files (or
microfilms) of local newspapers. Sometimes newspaper offices have
files of their own past editions and those of other local newspapers
they have absorbed. Especially from the mid-nineteenth century
local newspapers can be a fund of useful information and illustration.
If collections have been indexed this will enhance their value, and
local education authorities and library committees might well be
encouraged to finance such indexing where it has not been done. Even
if no index exists, however, intelligent searching around significant
dates will often yield reasonably quick returns.

The teacher will find maps an important source for local history and
one which children find attractive. Of published maps the most
accessible and useful are those produced by the Ordnance Survey,
and I shall touch on these in more detail later. Sufficient is it to say
here that most relevant OS maps for a region will be available in local
libraries. From the later eighteenth century local directories, general
and trade directories, guidebooks and travellers' descriptions are
fruitful and easy-to-use sources also commonly available in local
libraries in large numbers. Again I shall deal later with these and
other printed sources in more detail.

Thus without recourse to any but published works of one kind or
another the history teacher may acquaint himself with the history of
his region and gather a considerable array of primary sources to
illustrate and enrich his teaching. For those with limited time a
sufficient basis for good teaching of local history can be laid without
investigating manuscript material. For those who wish to go further,
however, collections of unpublished materials will certainly yield

invaluable material, and it is to be hoped that many history teachers, singly or in groups, will explore their potential.

If 'in service', WEA or university extra-mural classes dealing with local history and local records are available this may well be the most profitable way to begin. If not, a sensible first step would be a talk with the local county or borough archivist[5] to ascertain what catalogues and guides to the local collections exist, and to look through these and note the collections most likely to yield interesting teaching material. Guidance to the sort of material to look for is given in subsequent chapters. At the same time it is worth while to find out what the archivist's attitude is to visits by pupils and whether he is prepared to mount exhibitions or provide talks in school.

To start with it may be wise for the teacher to confine his activities to manuscripts dating from the sixteenth or even the seventeenth century, which are likely to be reasonably legible and often in English. Particularly worth investigating are documents illustrating topography, social conditions and other aspects of local life normally taught in school. Such records will include, for example, maps, especially enclosure maps, tithe records, wills and inventories, poor-relief records, election materials, school records, quarter-sessions records, local government records, gild records, charity records, parish registers, records concerned with communications (turnpikes, canals, railways, tramways, harbours) and public services, local diaries and scrapbooks, and records of local business firms, farms and estates. Even comparatively young children do not find the deciphering of manuscript material from the seventeenth century onwards too difficult, provided a little guidance is given, so that the teacher should have in mind the need to collect suitable documents of this period and to acquire some knowledge of the palaeographic technicalities involved in transcription.

Two problems are associated with older records. First, many were in Latin, and secondly the handwriting is very unlike modern script. More particularly, medieval Latin has a vocabulary and style often very different from classical Latin, and many documents utilize abbreviations and signs which make the Latin difficult for the uninitiated to follow even when the lettering is clear. It is very debatable whether most teachers should devote a great deal of time to mastering medieval Latin and palaeography unless they have a great urge to do so. For those who have time, inclination and a great deal of patience self-tuition is possible where no classes are available. The teacher who has some knowledge of classical Latin has an advantage, but both he and others will profit from a study, in conjunction with a standard school grammar, of Eileen Gooder's *Latin for Local History* (1961),[6] which gives some introduction both to the form taken by common types of medieval documents and also to medieval vocabulary. For anyone making any great use of medieval records, however, the possession of the *Revised Medieval Latin Word List* (ed. R. C. Latham, 1965) will be almost a necessity. This and C. T. Martin's *The Record Interpreter* (various editions) are likely to be available in the record offices where the documents are found. There are many good books which will give guidance to the beginner in reading older documents of which perhaps the best is L. C. Hector's *The Handwriting of English Documents* (1966).[7]

In my opinion, however, most teachers would be well advised to leave the use of original medieval manuscripts alone and to rely on printed translations. There are more important aspects of local history to master to become a successful teacher in this field. A teacher should not feel embarrassed before a class of schoolchildren at being unable to read and translate manuscripts seen, for example, on museum visits. The reading of medieval records is a highly specialized skill which many prominent professional historians do not possess, and children should be made aware of this, though they may be familiarized with the look of such documents.

A half-way house is for the teacher to master, by means of comparing transcripts and translations, or with the aid of a willing archivist or other specialist, a few significant documents and records, such as, for example, a local borough charter, or the local entries in Domesday, which he can use in class with his pupils. Classwork of this kind should be limited, however, for it soon loses the initial attraction of novelty. An eleven-year-old's verdict following introductory work in palaeography—'I prefer doing work on the Romans because every lesson you learn something different. In palaeography you do the same thing every time and in the same style'—should stand as a warning.[8]

What is necessary, however, where printed translations or transcripts of medieval records are used, is that the teacher should become familiar with the technical vocabulary of the past. He should know what is meant by a carucate, a virgate, view of frankpledge, fee farm, a sokeman, and so on. It is surprising how much can be discovered even from the *Shorter Oxford English Dictionary*.[9]

County and city record offices contain the official records of local government through the ages and of *ad hoc* authorities like school boards, together with much deposited material, particularly miscellaneous private collections. Sometimes ecclesiastical records have been deposited there too, though these may also be found in separate diocesan depositories. Local record offices are, of course, only one of the sources for the unpublished materials relating to the history of a region. National depositories, such as the Public Record Office (for the records of central government) and the British Museum, with its large miscellaneous collections, contain much material which will shed light on the history of provincial towns and villages. The professional writer of local history will often need to visit these repositories, but in most cases it would be unrealistic to expect teachers, even in the London area, to spend time in them. The time and expense involved would be disproportionate to the gain. What teachers can do to derive value from the national collections is to use published transcripts and calendars of certain collections (such as the PRO Calendars), some of which are very full, or to make use of easily obtained photographic reproductions. Some local libraries, for example, have obtained microfilms of nineteenth-century census schedules for their area. Most record depositories and libraries have facilities for photocopying documents and books, and copies of original Domesday extracts and tithe maps and schedules, for example, may be obtained from the Public Record Office.[10] Many local libraries have large collections of old photographs of life in their region, and teachers should make themselves familiar with these, and with publications which make use of them.

As well as printed, manuscript, cartographic and photographic records the teacher of local history will need to include in his preparation a survey of physical remains of the past—historic buildings of various kinds, archaeological sites, constructions like canals and railways, and industrial relics. He will need to visit them, to read about them, and to select those likely to be most valuable for teaching purposes. The content of local museums and the facilities offered by school museum services should also be included in the preliminary work.

Only after these preparations, which cannot be achieved overnight, will the teacher really be able to tackle the teaching of local history in a significant way. But the process of accumulating knowledge and expertise should continue throughout his career.

Teaching units and resource centres

Since the war volumes of collections of local records, or extracts from records illustrating aspects of local history, have been published for some counties to provide materials for teachers. These supplement what may be found in local record society publications and have the advantage of being chosen with children in mind, being suitably edited, with accompanying notes, and usually topically arranged. Thus we have, to give a few examples, the volumes of *English History from Essex Sources*, *Kentish Sources*, and, for Staffordshire, *Local History Source Books*. More recently many bodies and institutions, stimulated initially by the pioneer work of G. R. Batho at Sheffield, have produced collections of records relating to the local history of their areas, in facsimile or transcript form, for direct use in the classroom. Some enlightened local government authorities have officers attached to record offices with a special responsibility for sponsoring and producing such 'kits'. This development is part of the general movement for introducing pupils to original historical sources, and the many commercially produced teaching units on aspects of general history are well known. The best collections, local or general, contain not only facsimiles of records but informative notes for the teacher, bibliographies and suggestions for the use of the items in the classroom.

Those wishing to include local history in their syllabuses should certainly acquaint themselves with any of these collections which illustrate the history of their area,[11] for often these offer copies of records which are dispersed and difficult to locate. For documents in Latin or otherwise difficult to read they provide translations and transcripts. In class they can be used in a variety of ways, both in teaching national and purely local history. Class, group or individual exercises can be set based on individual records or combinations of different items and involving selection and other historical techniques. They can, too, be used as illustrative material during a teacher's exposition, and to make a classroom exhibition. It is difficult, however, for compilers to suggest uses that are suitable for all children likely to use the collections. Pupils' abilities and ages will vary considerably. They will be in different schools and districts, taught by teachers with varying interests, and following differently structured syllabuses. Consequently suggestions for class use tend to be very generalized, and some teachers incline, therefore, to use the facsimiles only for exhibition purposes. Where items are made the basis of classwork those teachers insufficiently knowledgeable about the nature of the archive classes to which the documents belong tend to set simple 'comprehension' exercises. Local history teaching units cannot be fully exploited unless the teacher is well versed in the general history of the region and has some notion of the sort of evidence that may be derived from the more important types of source. Moreover most local kits are based on the county, so as to cater for a large number of schools, and not especially on individual towns or villages.

Teachers should, therefore, regard such kits as useful aids but will need to have more first-hand involvement with the materials of local history if they wish to use it properly. If possible they should seek to gear their own collections specially to their particular locality. Then they will be able to provide what will exactly suit their own pupils, the syllabus they are following and the topics they have chosen. Moreover only by involving themselves in reading, searching, selecting, editing and thinking out class exercises will they achieve a real insight into the nature of the local history of the region and of its source material in relation to the needs of the pupils. Subsequent chapters are designed primarily to help teachers find suitable materials for themselves with general guidance on the sort of ways in which they can be used. Two sorts of local history source collections may be compiled: well structured 'units' on different aspects of the history of the locality or unstructured 'data banks'.

In compiling a teaching unit teachers should bear in mind the ages and abilities of the children for whom it is designed, and if a wide age and ability range is envisaged they will need to include items of varying degrees of complexity. They must decide, too, whether the kit is to illustrate the history of the region, the town, or a smaller area, and this will depend partly on the pupils for whom it is intended but also on the nature of the topic itself. It will have to be decided whether, as well as the essential explanatory notes for the teacher, background information and bibliography, they wish also to provide any secondary material for the pupils or whether the components should be confined entirely to copies of primary source materials. Special care is necessary in the selection of the records for reproduction. Apart from clarity and legibility in all kinds of facsimiles, variety is essential. To manuscripts and printed records should be added, where relevant, maps, pictures, photographs, diagrams, handbills, posters and so on. No one type of record should predominate. Too many newspaper extracts, for example, or too many maps, should be avoided. Written or printed items should not be too lengthy. Editing should be considered in certain cases, as well as the provision of notes and glossaries adapted to the type of children. If

documents are in Latin or a difficult hand, translations and trans-
scripts should be provided. Not all records need be reproduced
facsimile. Typescript or printed versions will often suffice and may be
preferred in some cases for ease of use. A proportion of facsimile
items in each collection will, however, make it more interesting and
attractive to the eye and indicate the physical nature of historians'
materials. General ideas for class use can also be included, and in
some cases actual exercises and work cards devised.

It may be that specialist historians or groups of teachers including
subject specialists will find it easier than others to construct kits of
this type for mutual use. Many non-specialist teachers may feel less
able to tackle the task, and both they and for that matter history
teachers generally may prefer to be involved with experts—including
archivists and librarians—in building up a large-scale local history
or environmental studies 'data bank'. Such a bank would include
original source materials in the form of facsimiles and transcripts of
records, photographs and maps, but also information sheets each
providing summaries of information on a separate local topic—a
particular building, medieval agriculture, travellers' descriptions, and
so on—and including a bibliography and indications of relevant
examples of records in the 'bank' and elsewhere. In addition there
should be teaching aids relating to aspects of local life, such as charts,
maps, diagrams, sets of statistics, sketches, and maybe tape recordings, slides, transparencies and film strips. Suggestions for activities
for children could also be included, both arranged by topics and
related to individual records and groups of records.[12] Such resource
centres may be built up for and kept within an individual school, with
access for pupils as well as teachers and associated with the school
library. If so they will need to be on a modest scale because of the
work involved in maintenance, and it is probably best that there
should be a single resource centre associated with the school library
where reprographic equipment is available, rather than a number of
banks associated with different departments. Economic considerations, among others, however, suggest that a large-scale resource
centre based on a teachers' centre, reference library, college of
education or the like, and serving all the schools of the district, is to
be preferred.[13] This could, of course, be accessible directly only to
the teachers and not their pupils. With a large-scale local studies or
local history bank in such a centre elaborate referencing will be both
desirable and possible. Individual items will need to be filed and
catalogued in such a way as to make them readily accessible for use

in different combinations to meet the varying needs of different teachers.[14] And, of course, facilities for reproducing the items to take away will be essential. In centres it will be easier for expensive reprographic equipment and facilities for tape recording, typing, photography and so on to be provided for teachers, and local education authorities should feel that such a service is worth funding. In such centres, too, the organization of teachers' 'workshops' and co-operation with other experts will be less difficult than in the case of individual schools. It would, of course, be possible for smaller collections of resources duplicated from the central resource centres to be based in individual schools, and some form of retrieval system might be devised so that pupils had indirect access to the central bank.

Yet it must be emphasized that however useful kits and resource banks are, most teachers, and especially history specialists in secondary schools, would be wise not to rely exclusively on them. The best resource centre for teacher and pupils still remains the library, and children should be brought up to use libraries. The danger that over-use of teaching units and resource centres will lessen the use of libraries and of reference books by children should be avoided, as too should be the impression that adult historians find their information in such synthetic institutions as 'information banks'.

For notes to this chapter see pp. 165–6.

4 Local history in its own right: I

Although every parish, village, town, county or region shares in the national story, each locality also has its own particular history, related to and interwoven with national history in various degrees maybe, but not identical with that of other places. Indeed, within Britain there were enormous varieties. Thus the experience of Sussex in the eighteenth century was very different from that of Lancashire or the West Riding in many particulars. Moreover enterprises or developments of little or no consequence nationally might well be extremely significant in the history of a particular locality: although the shipping of south-west England was of limited national importance in the nineteenth century, it was vital to the local economy. Not all aspects of such local history, however, are equally suitable for school syllabuses. In this chapter I suggest some of the topics which can often prove useful for study in school as purely local history, whether as part of history syllabuses or as elements of environmental or social studies, and to stress particularly types of primary source material and works of reference which may be available for use by teacher and pupil. Of course, a great deal of information may be obtained from secondary histories of particular areas, but it would clearly be impossible for these to be dealt with here, since they would differ for each locality. The teacher will, however, have these also in mind when embarking on any of the topics detailed below. Some of the subjects and sources dealt with in Chapters 6 and 7 (on aspects of national history which can be illustrated by local examples) will also be of value for the study of local history in its own right—and equally some of the themes developed in this chapter and the next might also be used in illustrating national history.

Early settlement: place names and physical remains
The paucity of easily understood sources and the need for specialized knowledge renders the peculiarly local history of a district for medieval and pre-medieval times less suitable for children than for

later periods. Nevertheless there will be certain topics which can be appropriately treated. The history of early settlement, for example, can be studied through the medium of place names and of fieldwork, while study of the geographical structure of the area will form a necessary basis not only for early history but for subsequent periods too.

Unless he is unusually well informed the teacher should approach the use of place names in the teaching of early settlement with caution, for amateurish guesswork can be very dangerous. There are a number of works to which initial recourse may be made, but the appropriate volumes of the English Place Names Society county series are, if published for the area concerned, the best starting point. Using information culled from these, from E. Ekwall's *Concise Oxford Dictionary of Place Names* (1960 edition), or other such works,[1] and from articles published in local historical society transactions or local monographs, the teacher will be in a position to guide his pupils in the use of place names to be found on modern large- or small-scale OS maps. The names of towns, villages, hamlets, farms, fields, natural features, roads, streets and districts may all give clues to early settlement and indeed to later history.

Celtic names, for example, prolific in Wales and parts of western England, become less numerous as one moves eastwards, though their existence will indicate settlement before the Anglo-Saxon invasions. Names deriving from the Roman occupation are perhaps the easiest to distinguish and will usually be well known locally. The extent of Anglo-Saxon settlement can be plotted on maps by noting, for example, the 'tons', 'hams', 'ings' and 'fords', and in certain parts, especially in the north and Midlands, evidence of Norwegian and Danish settlement can also be discovered by children searching out names containing, for example, 'garth', 'thwaite', 'by' and 'toft'. Sometimes place-name elements will yield more information than merely the existence of settlement, such as the nature of the settlement or ancient physical features connected with it. 'Burg' or 'burh' may indicate a fortified camp; Headingley (Yorks.) was the 'leah' or meadow of the people led by one Hedde. The Celtic 'cryw' indicates a ford; the Scandinavian 'gil' a valley; Askwith (Yorks.) is old Norse for 'ash wood'.

Some place names may illustrate changes of later periods, and clues as to their nature. French names derive from the post-Conquest period and the advent of a new ruling class. Then the names of the new landowners were often added to Anglo-Saxon place names. Thus

Cheriton Fitzpaine (Devon) records the existence of a 'church farm' before the Conquest and its acquisition by the Fitzpaines, who we know held the manor in the thirteenth century. Elements like 'monk' and 'bishop' indicate obvious links with the Church. Medieval colonization may be recorded in names of farms and hamlets which recall the type of clearance, as when they contain elements like 'wood', 'venn' (fen), 'heath', 'marsh'. And in towns street and district names may enshrine evidence of the past.

A teacher armed with a sound knowledge of the place-name history of his area has the raw material for a variety of lessons, and he will find that children of most ages respond well to work involving place names. Children from six or seven years find the search for 'ings' and 'hams' 'thwaites' and 'thorpes' absorbing. Junior-school children generally will find excitement in a 'treasure hunt' approach using sketch maps specially prepared by the teacher. Older children can work with more detailed maps, including the OS, and useful 'detective' exercises can be devised. The different types of place names in an area, for example, can be listed, then plotted on sketch maps made by the pupils, perhaps using different colours for different types of name. Not only is such activity a useful introduction to the significance of place-name study in the history of local settlement, and practice in deduction and recording, but it can also form the basis for imaginative work—for example, on the Anglo-Saxon or Danish invasions. It could also be used as an introduction to wider studies, such as Viking ships, Anglo-Saxon village life, the Norse sagas, and to model making, though these, of course, will not be peculiarly local.[2]

Physical remains of prehistoric and later periods are also obvious sources for the study by children of early and medieval settlement. These are dealt with in Chapter 8, which should be referred to in conjunction with this section. It may be noted here, however, that the OS period maps for particular areas are of great use not only for fieldwork but for work in the classroom. There is a map of *Ancient Britain* in two sheets (North and South) on which are marked over a thousand of the major visible antiquities, classified by ages from the Stone Age to the Dark Ages. Another, *Britain in the Dark Ages*, in a single sheet, covers the period 410 to the death of Alfred. Different coloured symbols indicate Celtic, pagan and Christian Anglo-Saxon features so that those areas which remained under Celtic control and those which passed to the Anglo-Saxons can be clearly discerned. More detailed maps for specific areas include *Southern Britain in the Iron Age*, which covers the period from the beginning of the fifth century B.C. to the middle of the first century A.D., *Neolithic South Wales, Neolithic Wessex, Celtic Earthworks of Salisbury Plain* and the *Trent Basin* (neolithic).

For the Roman period we have another single sheet map—*Roman Britain A.D. 43–410*. This is extremely useful for the teacher. It shows the roads, the different kinds of Roman towns and other settlement, temples, shrines, barrows and mausolea, villas, bath houses, other substantial buildings and remains, potteries, kilns, mines and quarries, forts, fortresses and fortlets, signal stations, camps, lighthouses, milestones, aqueducts, canals and frontier works, and has a topographical index, introduction and notes. Further information on important sites can be found in the transactions of historical and archaeological societies. Very useful here is Wilfred Bonser's *Romano-British Bibliography (55 B.C.–A.D. 449)* (Alva, 1964) much of which is topographically arranged. Works on Roman roads are touched on below. The use of this wealth of information for pupils' map work, fieldwork, modelling, diagrammatic representation, and the compilation of local gazetteer booklets and other productions and wall displays by groups of children is obvious. The work could not, however, be understandable except in a context of the general study of, for example, the Roman army, Roman road making, Roman town life and so on.

Topography

For both early and later periods a study of the physical background is essential to an understanding of local history, and historical aspects of topography are an important part of environmental and local studies. On the one hand the physical appearance of many heavily populated parts of the country has changed very considerably; on the other, even for very recent times, the basic geographical features remain very apparent. The topography of an area embraces both the basic physical structure and the changes wrought by man. Often our ancestors have bequeathed a physical legacy never to be entirely obliterated and which has shaped and influenced later history. The landscape and the townscape are, therefore, not unfrequently tangible palimpsests, the proper reading of which can tell us much about the historical development of an area.

The history teacher, and even more the teacher of environmental or local studies, must, however, beware of historical explanations deriving entirely from geographical evidence and of treating the historical development of a locality in too parochial a fashion. G. H. Bantock, writing about such popular school projects as 'our town', gives a salutary warning: 'The significance of the specific information within each field (history, geography, etc) will take its meaning to a considerable extent from its relation to other facts within the same field. Thus we sometimes hear it said that "our town" gained its specific historical importance from, say, its geographical position on a river. But such historical importance is by no means explicable solely in terms of geographical position. There will be a chain of historical occurrences which will have led to the foundation of a town on just that spot at that time. Thus the answer to the question "Why did 'our town' become a market town in the fourteenth century?" is not "Because it stood on a river", though such a position may have been a contributory factor, but because a series of events have occurred within the field properly to be termed historical processes which have led to its foundation at just that time.'[3]

An understanding of these events can be obtained only through a study of general 'historical' development rather than through a purely geographical approach. Historical development embraces economic, social and political factors too. That said, however, a knowledge of the geography and geology of the area remains a necessity for a proper comprehension of local history generally and of topography in particular. Climate, soil, structure and relief, for example, influence the type of farming; the presence of coal and minerals, of navigable waterways, of natural routeways and harbours will have helped to determine regional economic development. Here the OS maps and the maps of the Geological Survey will be invaluable. The Geological Survey maps are published in various scales by the Ordnance Survey for the Institute of Geological Sciences. Of these the quarter-inch-to-one-mile maps (being replaced by 1:253440) are the most useful for detailed work.[4]

The study of topography, an important aspect of all lines of local studies, however, goes further than geography. It involves the study of the impact of the past on the visible and tangible environment as well as the study of how a landscape or townscape differed in the past. It can make use of a large variety of graphic and pictorial materials of a kind often more attractive to children than purely written or printed records. It can be connected with formal and informal field-work, linking the concrete reality of the world outside the classroom with the history being studied. The element of detective work and the variety of the sort of clues available can make this area of local history particularly interesting for schoolchildren, as well, of course, as for adults.

In studying the topography of an area it is often best to start from the present scene and to work backwards, and often the 'then and now' approach will be most effective in the classroom. The teacher will need to be familiar with the various types and editions of OS maps. The most recent one-inch-to-the-mile (or its metric successor, 1:50,000) will be useful for large areas, but the 6 in. and the 25 in. maps will be needed too, especially for the examination of smaller areas. These modern maps will certainly yield clues on the past history of the area to the trained eye.[5] But they should often perhaps be used in conjunction with the first edition of the 1 in. map, for most parts of the country completed between 1805 and 1840. The publishers David & Charles reprinted this edition in 1969 (ed. J. B. Harley), with introductory notes on dating and interpretation for each sheet, and this should be invaluable for teachers. It is possible, too, to obtain from the map room of the British Museum copies of the original editions of large-scale maps (variously 2 in., 3 in., 6 in.) on which this 1 in. edition was based.[6] From 1840 there are earlier editions of 6 in. maps and from 1857 25 in. plans for all but waste and mountainous districts. A useful and cheap introduction to these is the *Historian's Guide to Ordnance Survey Maps* (National Council of Social Service, 1964), which shows the dates of the maps for each area. Local libraries will usually have copies of these. Some may also have large-scale town plans of 5, 10 or 10·56 ft to the mile, for the OS surveyed many towns to produce such plans in the period 1843–94. These show minute details not only of the dimensions of individual houses but even down to pumps, taps, privies, lamp posts, boilers, church and chapel pew arrangements, garden paths and summer houses. Thus the OS maps and plans alone can be used to illustrate a century or more of change—the growth of built-up areas, the construction of railways, roads, airfields and docks, the existence of large buildings like churches, factories and civic offices can all be seen, and the disappearance of parks, estates, farm land, forest and moor all traced. Moreover, since this was a period when directories and photographs can add further dimensions, a wealth of material exists for a teacher and his classes who wish to reconstruct in detail their locality in Victorian times.

Map study can be taken back further in time, too.[7] Pre-dating the first edition of the OS map may well be a tithe redemption map. Mainly as a result of an Act of 1836 tithe was commuted to a money rent in many English and Welsh parishes. In the process large-scale maps were made (varying from 27 in. to 13 in. per mile). Since parishes differ in area the actual maps vary enormously in size. They show, in great detail, usually for the period 1836–51, the physical features of the area, including roads and other communications, field boundaries, woods, heaths, waterways, houses, churches and other buildings. Each tithable plot of land is numbered and keyed to an accompanying schedule which indicates the names of the owner and occupier, the area of each plot and the new rent charge, the use a building was put to (barn, stable, mill, etc) or land use (usually as meadow, pasture, wood, orchard, garden, plantation, etc). Three contemporary copies were made. The one lodged now at the Public Record Office should certainly be available, and photocopies may be purchased. The copies originally placed with the diocesan records and the parish records may be available locally.

Though they exist for some 12,000 parishes, and some 80 per cent of the area of England and Wales, these large-scale tithe maps are not, however, universally available because in some places tithe had already been extinguished previously by a parliamentary enclosure which gave the priest a plot of land in lieu. Whether or not this was so there may exist for many places, especially in the Midlands, parliamentary enclosure maps, usually of the late eighteenth to mid-nineteenth centuries. Enclosure did not always involve all the common land in a parish. Sometimes only an acre of marsh was involved; sometimes the whole farming area of a village. The maps vary, too, sometimes showing only the area enclosed, sometimes the whole parish. Occasionally there is a map showing the pre-enclosure pattern of the village. Usually, however, there is only one map, showing the new landscape with varying amounts of detail, but usually on a large scale, the farms and allotments with the general physical features of the area. As with the tithe maps, a key indicates the owners of each plot of land. Since enclosure often marked a considerable change in the local topography, the maps are of great significance. Unfortunately there is no central depository for them. They are most likely to be found in local record offices, and local archivists and librarians will know of their existence, and may well have prepared lists of them.

OS, tithe and enclosure maps will, then, provide a basis for topographical study, perhaps going back to the late eighteenth century. It is less likely that other early detailed maps will exist to help the teacher, but for rural areas there may be some estate maps, contemporary with tithe and enclosure maps or predating them. These vary in their detail, but are usually valuable, especially when they are the first available map of an area. Often they will show the layout of manor house, farms, outbuildings, park, church, fields, tracks, lanes, roads, bridges, fords, toll gates, and in some cases provide evidence of early enclosure.[8] Some will show land use—arable, meadow, pasture, wood, heath, moor, orchard, gardens, and so on—and indicate ownership and tenancy. When the village is included the main buildings will be shown and perhaps smithies, brick kilns, gravel pits, tanyards, mills and like places indicated. Many of these maps are still privately held, others are in local record offices, which may anyway have photocopies of those not actually physically deposited. Some counties have published catalogues of estate maps. Glebe terriers (Chapter 5) may give additional information, particularly for the seventeenth century.

Enclosure, tithe and estate maps may exist for urban as well as rural areas, and these can be useful for showing the impact of industrialization and the transport revolution and for providing reliable street plans. From Tudor times onwards there exist general town plans for many places, and for the eighteenth century many of these are extremely detailed and accurate. Many eighteenth-century town plans were insets in the new county maps of the period, and in the nineteenth century many appeared in guide books and local histories. Local historians will know of these and other maps and plans and whether there are recent reproductions. In the nineteenth century large-scale plans of public utility and local government schemes for such developments as drainage, water supply, roads, rivers, canals, railways, tramways, docks and harbours and so on were usually made when Acts of Parliament were sought. The originals are at the House of Lords Record Office,[9] but copies may be available locally. Caution in their use is needed, since they were often anticipatory, and actual development may not have followed or may have taken place differently. Planning departments of local government authorities have many recent plans, copies of some of which can be procured by teachers. Occasionally plans of urban landowners and housing development schemes for the period from the eighteenth century may be available locally.

Maps and plans are attractive and useful materials for classroom use. Other attractive topographical sources, particularly for towns, are pictures and photographs. Many local libraries, record offices, societies, newspapers and individuals have already built up photographic collections, and the teacher should get to know them, for they add a further dimension to literary and cartographic sources.[10] They are, of course, useful for a much wider variety of topics than merely topography. Old picture postcards and reproductions of such cards are also valuable. Air photographs, too, may be obtained from various places;[11] the National Monuments Record (Fielden House, College Street, London S.W. 1) has a large topographical collection of photographs of buildings, and copies may be obtained.

On the whole maps, plans and pictures are best suited for class work dealing with the eighteenth century onwards. It would, of course, be difficult to list all the ways they could be used, but some can be suggested.[12] An interesting exercise, for example, is the reconstruction of a nineteenth-century high street by combining information from maps, plans and pictures with that from directories and guidebooks, which contain much on the topography and amenities of the places they cover. If such sources are sufficiently abundant and detailed it may well be possible for a class of junior or younger secondary-school children to construct a detailed plan of the street showing what shopkeepers and other persons occupied different parts. Some of the buildings may well be still standing, for others photographs may be available. Then elevated drawings of sites and sectors of the street may be constructed by groups or individuals. Younger children will enjoy the translation of the information into graphic wall friezes, and classes of all ages to fourteen or fifteen can profitably reconstruct the street in cardboard or other modelling materials.[13] In some places, as at Leeds and York, museums include reconstructed streets or individual shops and houses to illustrate past periods, and if these are visited as part of the exercise understanding will be enhanced.

The study of older maps and plans will give clues to the whereabouts of activities since gone, and sometimes there are physical remains. Old collieries and their railway communications, disused quarries, old ironworks and mills may be brought to light and serve to explain hitherto puzzling physical features, or to bring to life the textbook description of the past economy of the town or district. Likewise the chapel that has since passed through the stages of being a cinema, a bingo hall or a storehouse can be detected. The substantial row of town dwellings that are now solicitors' offices, and the mews converted into flats and garages, will be seen in a new light. All this can lead to explanations by the teacher and to investigations by the class in the library. Why, for example, were there so many chapels when there was a smaller population? Such work will serve to provide pupils with a greater insight into the topography of their district and its relationship to general local history. When they walk through their town they will do so with the seeing eye of greater awareness, their local roots will be strengthened and their historical sense stimulated.

Ordnance Survey, enclosure, tithe and other maps and plans can also be used for children to record and present by means of diagrams, graphs and plans features of the changing topography of a district and landscape. A series of plans or overhead projector transparencies can, for example, illustrate the expansion of the built-up area of a town, and this may be paralleled by graphs or block diagrams showing the size of the population, taken from the census reports. The relationship between old field boundaries and modern roads and building plots can be shown on contrasting maps; past and present land use can be graphed by older children. And even younger children can, with guidance in groups, produce contoured model maps showing the names and locations of old fields, lanes, farms, parklands, etc.[14] Maps can be used, too, to illustrate (or to discover) the reasons why modern roads take certain directions, the impact of the construction of a railway through a town centre, the effect of local transport services on the growth of residential, industrial and shopping areas, and so on.

Many of these exercises will lend themselves to some fieldwork and observation on the ground, and in some cases, especially with regard to the recent past, the use of oral evidence may be invoked. Relatives and elderly inhabitants may through interviews or questionnaires be encouraged to recall topographical and other changes. Such activity will often result also in the production of physical evidence in the form of old photographs, picture postcards, newspaper cuttings and so on. For those older children in many of our large towns who follow environmental or social studies syllabuses, study of the effects of wartime bombing, post-war reconstruction, slum clearance and general urban renewal can be deepened by work on the types of sources described above—especially the plans and reports of local government planning, engineering and architects' departments, backed by council minutes and reports. These may be used in conjunction with sources on such topics as population, local government structure and industrial development (dealt with in later chapters).

Secondary-school pupils in particular should be encouraged not only to see, to record and to present but also to explain orally (as in short talks, discussions, reports) and in continuous written prose.

Both straightforward narrative and explanation and imaginative work can derive from a study of local historical topography. Changes in a town based on the evidence of maps, for example, can be dealt with by a straightforward essay, or as seen through the eyes of an old man looking back over eighty years or so.

Imaginative exercises may also be helped and stimulated by the use of more literary types of evidence, though these will, of course, provide information which can be used in a more straightforward way too, often in conjunction with maps, plans and directories. The following extracts from a topographical description of Newcastle upon Tyne in 1649 is clearly invaluable for providing class material for the study of topography, industry and trade, and of town life generally:[15]

> Now let us describe unto you the other streets and markets in this town. First of the Sand Hill, a market for fish, and other commodities; very convenient for merchant-adventurers, merchants of coals, and all those that have their living by shipping. There is a navigable river and a long key or wharf, where ships may lie safe from danger of storms and may unload their commodities and wares upon the key. In it, are two cranes for heavy commodities, very convenient for carrying of corn, wine, deals, etc. from the key into the water-gates, which are along the key-side, or into any quarter of the town.
>
> In this market-place are many shops and stately houses for merchants, with great conveniences of water, bridge, garner, lofts, cellars and houses of both sides of them. Westward they have a street called the Close. East, the benefit of the houses of the key-side.
>
> In this Sand-hill standeth the town-court, or guildhall, where are held the guilds every year by the mayor and burgesses, to offer up their grievances, where the mayor keepeth his court every Monday, and the sheriff hath his county-court upon Wednesday and Friday. . . . Under the town-court is a common weigh-house for all sorts of commodities. King Henry the Sixth sent to this town, as to other cities and towns, brass weights according to the standard. Near this is the townhouse, where the clerk of the chamber and chamberlains are to receive the revenues of the town for coal, ballast, salt, grind-stones, etc. Next adjoining is an alms-house . . .

The nature and whereabouts of other useful contemporary descriptions of travellers and topographies are dealt with below. Topographical information for early modern times may be culled from such records as quarter-sessions rolls and books, which have often been published by local societies and provide details on road maintenance and bridge construction and repair. Manorial court rolls may mention buildings, roads and fields, borough council minutes will contain references to highways and important buildings, docks, market places and the like. On the whole, however, topographical information in such records is likely to be too fragmentary to make its use in school very fruitful or easy. The assiduous teacher with time to spare, however, might well collect together evidence from these sources, and perhaps, too, from other records such as monastic suppression or dissolution papers and glebe terriers, to make a composite information sheet on which class work could be based.

For the nineteenth century a great deal of topographical information is to be found in parliamentary papers. In particular may be mentioned the boundary reports of 1831–2, 1837 and 1888,[16] all of which contain not only excellent maps and plans but much descriptive and statistical information. The report of 1837 is particularly full of information not only on topography. It includes for each town described, as well as a map, the names of the streets with the number of houses and their total and average value. Sometimes the number of ratepayers in different categories in each street is given.

The topography of larger areas than the village or town is best studied by means of OS and other large-scale maps. The early maps of such cartographers as Saxton (coloured copies from HMSO), Norden and Speed are of limited value and show roads only sparsely if at all. They are, however, very attractive to children and they do illustrate such features as parklands, bridges and churches, and show early spellings of place names. Sometimes they have marginal plans of towns.

On the whole, however, topography on the county or regional scale is best dealt with as part of the history of local communications, and the sources described below in connection with the development of transport and communications will therefore be the most appropriate.

Communications and transport

The importance of regions and towns in the past, as today, is often reflected in and influenced by the means of communication available and man's attempts to improve them. The history at various periods of roads and road transport, river navigation, canals, railways, and shipping and port facilities are topics of considerable importance in some areas, and of significance in many, and where they are not important their very absence may need comment and investigation.

The sources the teacher will find useful for roads and tracks in early times are largely physical or secondary.[17] Early trackways can be investigated by making use of the OS period maps. For Roman times we have, as well as the OS map mentioned earlier in this chapter, I. D. Margary's *Roman Ways in Britain* (revised edition 1967), and for particular areas Margary's *Roman Ways in the Weald* (1965 edition) and *Roman Roads in the South East Midlands* by the 'Viatores' (1964), both extremely detailed topographically arranged works.

For the seventeenth and eighteenth centuries there are road maps of the strip variety, not unlike those produced today by the Automobile Association. Of these the maps in the road book John Ogilby (Ogilvy)'s *Britannia* (1675) (facsimile reproductions by Duckham, 1939) are the best known. They indicate the main topographical features to be observed by travellers, including important houses, churches, bridges, mills and so on. Children of different ages can use these (and, indeed, other maps) as the basis of an imaginative description of a journey in the form of letters, diaries or stories. They form an excellent basis, too, for younger children for the construction of class friezes and of project work, as, for example, the collection of information on the places and buildings and on the types of transport which would have been used. Another interesting exercise is to get children to draw alongside a copy of an Ogilby strip map a modern equivalent for the same route; or this can be the basis of model work. For the period from the eighteenth century onwards the teacher will be primarily interested in improvements of local communications by means of roads, canals and railways. For these topics the volume of material available to the research historian is considerable, and there are useful published guides to the various sources.[18] For this reason, and because many are difficult of access and too detailed for the teacher's purposes, I confine myself here to noting a few of the more pedagogically useful types.

Maps, of which I have already said something, are, of course, essential. From the mid-eighteenth century surveying techniques improved and there are many good county maps which pre-date the OS maps,[19] the earlier editions of which are themselves, of course, valuable. Literary sources provide entertaining comments on the unfortunate state of local roads in pre-turnpike times, and, it must be said, of some turnpikes too. The accounts of travellers often provide vivid teaching material. In 1788, for example, Wesley, journeying in Lancashire, wrote:[20]

> I went on through miserable roads, to Blackburn . . . through equally good roads we got on to Padingham . . . through still more wonderful roads to Haslingden. They were sufficient to lame any horses, and shake

any carriage to pieces—N.B. I will never attempt to travel these roads again. . . . We hobbled on to Bury, through roads equally deplorable.

The *General Views of Agriculture*, some of which are also available in modern reprints,[21] contain for each county brief sections on roads and sometimes comment on other means of communication. Local directories give details of coach and carrier services, and similar information on single notice sheets is often to be found in local record offices. Such advertisements can be used by children of the middle-school age range and older to deduce all sorts of aspects of contemporary travel, including passenger and freight charges, and the time taken for journeys. They can serve, too, as stimulus material for work on coach travel generally and the early history of the royal mail. Such advertisements usually make clear the importance of inns in the communication system of the pre-railway age and pupils can undertake further work using directories which list inns. Sometimes it may be possible by providing directories for different dates to lead children to deduce the decline in the number of inns which usually followed the introduction of a railway. Since the advertisements often give the routes to be followed, they can also form the basis for map work.

Freight rates to be charged by carriers were from 1691 fixed periodically by the JPs, and tables of these rates are to be found in quarter-sessions minute books (sometimes now published) or in single sheets, for they had to be posted in public places. Such extracts as the following (for Staffordshire, 1781)[22] can clearly be used for illustration or exercises:

Ordered that the rate of carriage of goods from London to the several places in this county be as followeth, that is to say for every hundred-weight

	Lady Day to Michaelmas £ s d	Michaelmas to Lady Day £ s d
To Lichfield Close, Walsall, Burton, Wolverhampton, Tamworth, Rugeley and places of like distance	5 6	6 0
To Stafford, Penkridge, Uttoxeter, Stone, Eccleshall, and places of like distance	6 0	6 6
To Newcastle, Cheadle, Leek and places of like distance	6 6	7 0

and so proportionately for a greater or less weight (except small parcels not exceeding ten points weight a penny per pound)

Until 1835 parish highway surveyors had the task of keeping non-turnpiked roads in repair, and their accounts can be revealing both of the materials used in road repair and of the system employed: some parishioners did their statutory manual labour on the roads, while others paid a composition or provided substitutes. The following extract from the accounts of the surveyors of Aveley (Essex) in 1807 is an example, from which older pupils could deduce the arrangements in practice there:[23]

Rents £	Inhabitants	Days' work	Composition £	6d in £ £ s d		
146	Sir Thos. Lennard, Bt.	12	46	1	3	0
400	Jos. Joyner	48				
115	Willis Finch	12	15		7	6
80	John Curtis	6	30		15	0
20	Thos. Bird	–	20		10	0
15	Widow Keeling	–	15		7	6
6	John Standish	–	6		3	0
6	John Simpking	–	6		3	0
5	Thos. Livermore	–	5		2	6
3	David Ashfield	–	3		1	6

The records of turnpike trusts include maps, plans, letters, schedules of charges, regulations of the types of traffic permitted, order and minute books, and finance accounts. Very occasionally a toll-house keeper's day book recording the passage of traffic will have survived. Printed copies of Acts of Parliament setting up the trusts may be found in the minute book. Original turnpike plans were deposited with the clerks of the peace (from 1792), so that they are often to be found in local record offices. Few turnpike records have been published, so that the teacher who wishes to make use of them will have to devote some time to sifting them for relevant teaching materials. If he does he will undoubtedly find some that will have a strong visual attraction while at the same time illustrating much about the system and about road travel and carriage generally in the locality.

The records of turnpike trusts are more likely to be found locally than those of canals or railways, the bulk of which are with the British Transport Historical Records (66 Porchester Road, London w2 6ET) The British Museum map room has a large number of canal plans.

For teachers unable to make use of such collections there is nevertheless a great deal of material. Apart from OS and other maps, dealt
with above, there may be available in large libraries such works as
J. Priestley's *Historical Account of the Navigable Rivers, Canals and
Railways throughout Great Britain* (1831), and John Phillips's *General
History of Inland Navigation* (1805 edition, republished 1970), which
contain maps and plans, and the maps produced by George Bradshaw.[24]

Railway construction often effected considerable topographical
changes, especially in the centres of large towns, where whole areas
of housing were sometimes swept away, bridges and embankments
built, and roads re-routed. Such changes can be discovered and
illustrated from local guidebooks, newspapers, OS and other maps
and large-scale plans deposited with local authorities at the time and
now often in local record offices. The study of such a disruption can
form an interesting project or exercise for a class of older secondary-
school children and can lead to all sorts of map work (especially of a
'before and after' type), fieldwork and descriptive accounts, and
might also be a preliminary to a similar investigation of recent urban
road building.

Local newspapers and directories will certainly contain information
on rail, road and canal transport, sometimes in the form of advertisements, which can create much interest in children. Old railway timetables, of which Bradshaw's are the best, contain not only train
schedules but also bus and coach connections.[25] By combining the
use of these with maps children can build up in plan or map form
the local communications system at various times in the recent past,
and perhaps compare it with the present situation. The decimation
of railway branch lines in the years since the Second World War and
the decline of the canals, followed by some recent resurrection for
recreational purposes, are worth while investigating and can involve
interesting fieldwork.

Parliamentary papers are, when available, mines of material. For
road communication the most useful are the report of the Royal
Commission on Roads (1840, xxvii) and the annual returns of turnpike trusts (for 1836–83). The latter show the income and expenditure
of the companies. For railways there are many papers, and W. R.
Powell's *Local History from Blue Books* (1969) would be worth
consulting before searching for them. For canals the report of the
Royal Commission on Canals of 1906–11 contains much information
and detailed maps. The following extract from that report could

clearly be used not only to illustrate, through the compilation of maps, the water communications of the region but also as a lead into a series of general lessons on the industry and trade of the region and on the history of communications generally.

Canals connected with the Humber, showing the
Principal towns en route

Goole to Leeds—Via Aire and Calder Canal, to Bradford, Keighley, Skipton, Nelson, Burnley, Blackburn, Chorley and Wigan; via Leeds and Liverpool Canal to Liverpool.

Goole to Manchester—Via Aire and Calder Canal to Wakefield, then by Calder and Hebble Navigation to Sowerby Bridge, and from there by Rochdale Canal to Manchester. There is another route by Huddersfield Canal, but this is too narrow and shallow.

Goole to York—Ouse River and on to Ripton by Ouse Navigation and Linton Navigation, and River Ure Navigation.

Goole to Pocklington—Via River Ouse, River Derwent and Pocklington Canal.

Goole to Malton—River Derwent Navigation.

Goole to Thorne—Doncaster, Rotherham, and Sheffield via Dutch River, River Don Navigation and Sheffield and Tinsley Canal.

Goole to Barnsley—1st route via Aire and Calder Canal and Barnsley Canal . . .

Of course, the teacher would be unwise to embark on the teaching of local communications without making himself familiar with recent secondary works. There is a plethora of material on railways; George Ottley's massive *Bibliography of British Railway History* (1966) and the volumes of *A Regional History of the Railways of Great Britain* (ed. D. St J. Thomas and C. R. Clinker) are particularly worth consulting. For canals the regional histories by George Hadfield are excellent.

Although communications in a particular age or as topic over a long period can provide a good subject for study, teachers will often find it useful to treat topography, industry and trade (see below) and communications together, for the materials overlap a great deal and the topics themselves are inextricably linked. These topics, too, are very suitable for comparative studies where one period is contrasted with another, including the present. Map work is usually basic to such studies, and children of different age groups can in different ways build up a series of comparative maps, plans or relief models. Once this has been done, enduring patterns of lines of communication and their relationship to the topography may be noted. The results of the introduction of new means of transport, and the influence on settlement and the growth of industry and trade may be worked out from the maps and related to tables of population figures, and the growth and decline of industries. Some places owed their existence to the railway—as Crewe and Middlesbrough; some were increased in importance—like Swindon; while yet others were bypassed and declined.

For junior-school children there is much scope in this area for making models and pictures—for example, of different types of roads, of railway stations, of canal wharves and barges—of aspects of the history of communications in the district. They can carry out a modern traffic census and compare the types of vehicles with those listed in local turnpike records. More ambitious work, too, is possible. An enterprising teacher could provide his class with copies of, for example, a list of tolls to be paid at various turnpike toll gates, an appropriate map, pages from one or more directories listing inns along the route. These could then be the basis for numerous individual or group exercises. A copy of the map might be made, and the inns and gates plotted. The number of inns could be compared with the number of hotels and inns now along the route (and it will be of interest if any of the original ones still survive). Lists of different kinds of animals paying toll could be made and questions on work cards answered about the sort of farming this indicates. The different types of waggons and carriages mentioned may be identified and searched out in reference books and directories, drawn and described. If there is a folk museum in the district there may be actual waggons extant. If any toll houses survive models can be made of them, and this might be used to stimulate some dramatic work based on the duties of the gatekeeper. If a traveller's description of this or another road in the district is available, it also could be used to stimulate imaginative work. Directories may be searched, too, for occupations concerned with road travel—not only carriers but coach makers, wheelwrights, those concerned with horses—and these can be listed and described.[26] In this way some conception of life without the internal combustion engine may be attained.

In lines of development approach in junior schools and the younger forms of secondary schools there is much scope for imaginative work based on roads. Thought might be given, for example, to the kinds of people who travelled along the roads of the district at different periods of time, how they were dressed, and their modes of transport. This might be extended to rail travel, too, and in this century to bus and car travel. Both picture and frieze work, as well as literary exercises, can develop from this and help to link the topic chronologically with other topics studied. In all this there would be plenty of opportunity for library investigations, use of sources and projects. One group of Liverpool teachers made a collection of materials on the Liverpool–Prescot–Warrington turnpike (1725–1871), which was so designed to enable work on the road's history (modelling, composition, reproduction, imaginative accounts, fuller general reading) to be undertaken by groups of different ability levels.[27]

With older children such topics as the interconnection between communications and the local economy may be illustrated by various exercises. They can, for example, plot on maps the position of factories and warehouses in relation to railway stations and canal wharves, and of rail and water routes in relation to topographical features, centres of population and industry, coal mines and so on. Pupils may be brought to understand the changing significance of different types of transport by, for example, compiling graphs and tables of figures showing mileages of turnpiked roads, of canals and of railways in the region at different times, comparing population figures of towns on the railway and those not, the frequency of train services compared with coaches (and later buses), and the growth of suburbs. The construction of Ogilby-type maps for railways and canals can be an interesting and informative exercise for pupils of various abilities. The census reports and directories will show whether railway growth affected the trades and industries in an area and group work relating the spread of the railway network to changes in occupations can be undertaken.

Both average and less able children can do useful and rewarding work in the production of a series of large-scale wall maps, to illustrate for example, the road system of a region at different dates, its navigable waterways, its railways and its docks and harbours. Or the same exercise may result in group loose-leaf booklets containing both maps, pictures, graphs and tables and written information. Picture postcards, photographs, newspaper cuttings and the like can all be used. Some teachers may be able to find the time for plaster or *papier-maché* landscape models to be made instead of maps, and though time-consuming much can be learnt by children in such a production.

There is, too, a great deal of scope for fieldwork in visiting canals and railways, looking at old wharves, at railway buildings, at the bridge building that both railways and canals resulted in, and other physical evidence. Links may be made with other aspects of industrial archaeology and the study of Victorian architecture.[28] A Surrey history teacher has described how with a class of thirteen-year-olds he linked classroom study (through maps and secondary works) of the geographical and economic background of the Basingstoke canal—land formation, size of population, land use, and location and type of industry—with fieldwork. The canal was examined *in situ*, and children collected information in accordance with instructions on work sheets, and they also visited a working lock at Chertsey. This led to a study of canals nationally and outside Britain, and the making of a tape recording on the history of the canal. Other activities by individuals grew out of all this, and the success of the whole venture stimulated the teacher to collect original documentary evidence on the canal for future use.[29]

For notes to this chapter see pp. 166–8.

5 Local history in its own right: II

Both junior and secondary-school syllabuses for history or allied subjects are likely to include some study of industry, agriculture, trade and occupations, and for these topics conditions in the pupils' own locality are naturally of particular interest. Most areas contain both towns and rural areas, though types of towns and countryside differ considerably from one part of the country to another.

Medieval and early modern industry and trade
The bulk of suitable sources for the purely local history of the occupations of townsfolk will be for the post-medieval period. For the Middle Ages such materials are scarcer and more difficult for both teacher and class to understand and make use of. Since it is often younger children who study the medieval period, such local records as are available for class use are better suited to illustrate the characteristics of town life generally rather than the special characteristics of a local town. For that reason medieval sources of this kind are dealt with in some detail in Chapter 6. In some cases, however, the sources examined there may be of use for purely local history, too.

Even for the Middle Ages and the early modern period there are, however, some uniquely local characteristics which can be illustrated for school purposes from suitable sources. About a third of the forty or so important medieval and Tudor towns and about half those in the Stuart period were seaports. There were also many other small maritime towns. Since land communications in those times were so poor, and since during these periods English overseas trade expanded, teachers in schools situated on or near the coast will certainly wish to study aspects of town history which distinguish ports from inland centres. The economy and life of some inland towns, however, was also geared to overseas trade and linked to the fortunes of near by, or in some cases distant, ports—this was particularly true of such woollen textile towns as Norwich, York, Leeds, Halifax, Bury St Edmunds, Salisbury, Winchester, Wells, Frome, Bath and Coventry.

And since the most important industry before the eighteenth century was undoubtedly the production of woollen and worsted cloth the study of towns in the three main areas of production—the West Country, East Anglia and Yorkshire—will necessarily involve investigation of the impact of that industry on the towns and their hinterland. The types of cloth made varied from area to area and sometimes from place to place within the area, and at certain times important new cloths were developed. Moreover the organization of the domestic woollen industry and trade also differed in the three main regions. The towns varied, too, some being market and finishing centres, others actually places of manufacture. Apart from the woollen industry, the mining of lead, copper, tin, salt and coal was significant in some areas, as were shipbuilding and metalworking in certain places. Contemporaries were well aware of and interested in such regional economic differences, and often, especially for the early modern period, travellers' and topographers' descriptions provide colourful, interesting and fruitful source material for introducing children to a study of their own district.

Celia Fiennes's account of how the local woollen cloth was fulled at Exeter in 1698[1] can hardly fail to stimulate interest. First, she wrote,

> they lay [the serges] in soack in urine then they soape them and soe put them into the fulling-mills and soe worke them in the mills drye till they are thick enough, then they turne water into them, and soe scower them; the mill does draw out and gather in the serges its a pretty divertion to see it, a sort of huge notch'd timbers like great teeth, . . . when they are thus scour'd they drye them in racks strained out, which are as thick set one by another as will permitt the dresser to pass between, and huge large fields occupy'd this way almost all round the town . . . then when drye they burle them picking out all knotts, then fold them with a paper between every fold and so set them on an iron plaite and screw down the press on them which has another iron plaite on the top under which is a furnace of fire of coales, this is the hott press; then they fold them exceeding exact and then press them in a cold press; some they dye . . . I saw the severall fatts [vats] they were a dying in, of black, yellow, blew and green—which two last coullours are dipped in the same fatt, that which makes it differ is what they were dipp'd in before, which makes them either green or blew . . .

Investigative work can be undertaken with directories, encyclopaedias and other reference books to find out what fulling was, how a fulling mill worked, and how cloth was fulled without a mill. In the West Country it may well be noticed that some children in the school will have the surnames Fuller or Walker, and the significance of them can be elucidated and other such names (as Webber, i.e. weaver) listed, too. Other words in the script may need discussion and perhaps the compilation of a glossary. Both junior and younger secondary-school children could draw strip 'cartoons' with captions to explain the different cloth-finishing processes. Examination of town plans and maps of Exeter will show the whereabouts of some of the tenter fields referred to by Celia Fiennes, and children will discover that some of these areas still bear their early names. This can lead to a study of the organization of cloth production in Devon and Somerset, with some comparison with other cloth areas. Probate inventories (see below) of clothiers' and others engaged in the trade could fill out the picture.

Celia Fiennes's book *Travels through England on a Side Saddle* is only one of several well known works of this kind.[2] They include Richard Blome's *Britannia* (also seventeenth-century), and for the sixteenth century William Camden's *Britannia* (reprinted 1974) and the *Itinerary* of John Leland. Some counties are lucky enough to have detailed contemporary accounts of their own of this kind, full of topographical, economic and social information. Thus there are, for example, William Lambard's *Perambulation of Kent* (1576), Richard Carew's *Survey of Cornwall* (1602) and William Dugdale's *Antiquities of Warwickshire* (1656). Children in the south-west peninsula may well be fascinated by Richard Carew's descriptions of the harbours of Cornwall, as when he compared the ports of Plymouth and the Fal in the words 'Falmouth braggeth that a hundred sayle may anker within its circuite and no one of them see the others tops, which Plymouth cannot equal'. Indeed, seaports and their trade have attracted the attention of many observers and travellers, who have often left graphic descriptions. The footnotes and bibliography in T. S. Willan's *The English Coasting Trade, 1600–1750* (1938)[3] will give a lead to many useful published sources of this kind.

Useful original records, too, may have been published by record societies or appear in modern histories. Thus a Huguenot Society publication includes letters from French refugees who took up residence in Norwich in the sixteenth century: Anaries and Anna van der Hughe wrote from Norwich to their parents in Ypres in 1567, imploring them to come to England with the rest of the family.[4] 'I and my brother will supply you with what you require here as a weaver, for there is a great trade doing.' Clement Baet wrote to his

wife, telling of his safe arrival in the Huguenot community of
Norwich, and told her that 'there is a good trade in bays and I will
look after a house as quickly as I can to get into business for then it
will be easy to make money. Bring all your and your daughter's
clothing, for people go well clad here . . . God give you the same
loving peace and riches as we have here at Norwich. It is very dear
to hear the word of God peacefully.'

Such extracts used as illustrations of local or national history are
clearly colourful and interesting. They would be useful, too, for
children studying East Anglian history, as a basis for deductive
exercises. They illustrate the prosperity of Norwich, why the refugees
came, their business ambitions, the types of cloth made, and so on.
They would form, too, both for junior and other children, a stimulus
for dramatic work and imaginative writing. Bald descriptions in
textbooks of the development of the production of 'new draperies'
would assume a greater reality.

The records of town government, which are discussed in some
detail in Chapter 6, can also be used to throw light on local industry,
and especially on the activities of town authorities and gilds and on
the markets and fairs which were then of such significance. In
particular the records of the entry of freemen can be analysed to show
dominant trades in a town. Some freemen's rolls have been published,
but the originals are not very difficult to use.[5] Simple analysis is quite
possible for children from ten upwards. The following extracts (1593)
showing entries at Exeter could easily be used to deduce that cloth
manufacturing in general and fulling (or tucking) in particular were
important there a century before Celia Fiennes's visit. They also
illustrate the various ways in which freedom could be attained—
by apprenticeship, following a father, or paying an entrance fee
(fine).[6]

Oct 15   John Smythe, tucker, apprentice of Thomas Martyne, tucker
          John Helliar, tucker, apprentice of Hugh Warren
          John Cater, glover, apprentice of Gregory Hunt
          George Hale, tucker, fine of £1
Oct 22   Thomas Brennocke, leather-dresser, fine of £1
          Michael Jacobe, tucker, fine of £1
          Richard Cornishe, weaver, apprentice of William Dodridge
Nov 26   John Levermore, sone of John Levermore, by succession

In maritime counties the study of sea-going trade, docks and
shipping will naturally form a part of the local history studied. For

the medieval and early modern periods the ups and downs of trade
and the types of goods dealt in can be illustrated from different sorts
of customs records. Some of these are purely statistical. For the
period of the late thirteenth to the mid-sixteenth centuries we have
recently published totals for wool and cloth imports for every
significant port, and the information is also given in the form of
graphs.[7] These show not only the volume of trade from time to time
but also the proportions in the hands of English merchants, Hanse
merchants or other foreigners. Such easily accessible material should
not be ignored by teachers.

Sometimes from medieval times even fuller records of the trade
carried on at ports is available in print. The following extract is an
example. It is a translation from the Bristol customs records (for
the year 1480)[8] which would be very suitable for class exercises.
Children could deduce from it Bristol's medieval trade connections
with Ireland and Iceland. Investigation of terminology would be
needed and perhaps the compilation of a glossary of such words as
'last', 'tun', 'wey' and so on. C stands for 'hundred'.

Date	Shipping particulars	Shipper	Cargo	Valuation for customs £	s	d
12 Feb.	Katerin of Milford Thomas Jorden' from Ireland	the master	17 C hake	8	10	0
			6½ barrels white herring	1	12	6
12 Feb.	Leonard of Bristol John Cogh to Iceland	Denis Bracy	6 weys malt	4	0	0
			12 tuns salt	10	0	0
			6 lasts flour	9	0	0
			12 barrels butter	6	0	0

Records of the shipments of goods paying national customs duties
are most likely to survive, however, for the period from 1565 into the
eighteenth century in the form of the port books. Where these have
been reproduced in print they will form good teaching material, and
even where they exist only in the original manuscript xerox copies
may be obtained; many are not too difficult to read, especially for the

years after 1660, when they are in English.[9] Not all are identical in form but most show the date, the name of the ship entering or leaving the harbour, the names of its home port and of its captain, its tonnage, the names of merchants shipping goods, and details of the goods.

More varied and often more vivid material on the history of ports can be found in such sources as the published volumes of the *Calendar of State Papers, Domestic* and *Acts of the Privy Council*, which large reference libraries will possess. In them are, for example, graphic details of piracy, smuggling, war at sea and the fortunes of trade generally, which make good teaching material. The *Calendar of State Papers, Domestic* for 1653, for instance, contains a very full petition from the merchants of Barnstaple to the government, bemoaning how their trade has been affected by Irish pirates, Prince Rupert's fleet, and French and Dutch warships. They complain that their Newfoundland fishing trade has been damaged by this and by widespread piracy in the Bristol Channel: 'so vexed and infested by the daily incursions of Brest and Dutch pirates, that we tremble to consider the impossibility of the return of that small remainder of our Newfoundland ships which are to be expected here two months hence, with the proceeds of 10 months labour, unless [you appoint] . . . some vessels to clear and secure the channel'. Such an extract could be used in class in several ways. As initial stimulus material it could lead into a study of the West Country merchants' interests in the Newfoundland fisheries and the whole fascinating organization of that trade, or into a study of seventeenth-century piracy with special reference to the West Country, on which there is much information. Or the organization and nature of the trade of the West Country ports generally could be studied. Project work, map work, and dramatic and imaginative exercises in these areas would not be difficult to devise for children of all ages.

This extract is printed in full; others are entered in the *Calendar* in an abbreviated form. Some brief entries may, however, suggest that it would be worth while to seek a xerox copy of the fuller original from the Public Record Office.

For some ports and other towns merchants' accounts and letters may have been published, and in the larger ports the records of trading companies. The published records of the York Merchant Venturers, the Merchant Adventurers of Newcastle upon Tyne and the Bristol Merchant Venturers contain much material not only on trade itself but on the development of port facilities.

Industry, trade and occupations from the eighteenth century
For more recent times there is a great variety of suitable material for
the study of local industry and occupations. The industrialization of
Britain from the later eighteenth century onwards is a basic ingredient
of school history at the national level. Yet, as is well known, different
regions were affected by industrial change in different ways. Once-
prosperous regions of rural domestic industry served by comfortable
market and trading towns reverted to purely agricultural areas and
the towns lost their significance, and even their population; other
areas once industrially less important sprang to the fore. The fortunes
of local industry in modern times—decline and disappearance as well
as emergence and growth—must therefore be valid topics for school
history in any part of the country. But though the history for different
places may be different, the types of source material are often similar.
   For the period from 1801 we have the published decennial censuses.
I mention these below as population sources, but they are for the
nineteenth and twentieth centuries the chief source of information on
the distribution and nature of local occupations over more than a
century and a half. Information from 1851 onwards is, however,
extremely detailed, and with all but the oldest pupils teachers will
usually need to make simplified extracts for class use. For the
censuses of 1841, 1851, 1861 and 1871 it is possible to obtain copies
of the original manuscript enumerators' books giving the occupation
of each individual in each dwelling. They can be used to show the
distribution of trades and crafts in different parts of the same town.
Published directories, too, can provide similar information for different years. Particularly useful are White's, Kelly's and the Post Office
directories. Those directories that pre-date or, as in the early nineteenth
century, provide greater detail than the censuses are especially valuable. Local directories, both general and trade, do not list all inhabitants, but they do name the most important inhabitants and
the tradesmen of various kinds, so that the dominant trades and industries can be deduced.
   Directories and information extracted from censuses can be used
in a variety of interesting ways by children. Directories often provide
as well as lists of tradesmen and others brief descriptive surveys of
local industries. Both younger and older pupils, individually or in
groups, may analyse the different trades and occupations in a village
or section of a town at one or more points of time. This can lead to
such exercises as a comparison of the occupations followed in the
same street or area at different times in the past and today. Similarly

the predominant trades for a whole town can be investigated, perhaps making use of the 'Yellow Pages' of the modern telephone directory for contemporary comparison. Used in combination with OS and other maps, industries, streets and buildings can be plotted on sketch maps. Evidence of now extinct crafts can stimulate visits to local museums to find physical evidence of such trades—their tools, their products and so on—and, if physical remains of works exist, an 'industrial archaeology' field study itinerary can be planned. The local reference library will perhaps need visiting, too, to seek out more information on the trades concerned, or the teacher may provide reference books in the classroom or reproduce copies of relevant pages out of them.

Older children can use a number of directories over a period, together with information from the printed censuses, to plot the introduction, growth and decline of local industries. Maybe these changes can be linked to the impact of transport changes (Chapter 4). The coming of the railways, for example, often caused a decline in the trades concerned with road transport. Railways, especially local lines, also created suburbs and attracted certain types of industry. The social and occupational structure of different parts of a town at different times can also be recorded in graphs, tables of statistics, maps or diagrams. Facsimiles of directories, and sometimes of census material, can form the basis for work cards with graded questions answerable from a study of the example. Some directories carry advertisements, often attractive and amusing to children, which can form the basis of imaginative work as well as being extremely in- formative. Practical activity may include the construction of models of some of the works or factories that feature in the advertisement, and wall friezes can be made to illustrate the occupations followed in different local streets at different times. For more recent times it may be possible for children to collect relics of dead or dying trades, for it is surprising what is still to be found in the homes of relatives and acquaintances. All such activities can form part of a more detailed survey in depth of an area by a class over an extended period, as an exercise either in history or in social or environmental studies, and including aspects other than occupations and industry.[10]

For children living near coastal areas the growth of seaside resorts is a feature of recent history which can be studied from local guide books and directories. Since the railways had much to do with this, the development of local rail services may be examined, using sources suggested elsewhere in the last chapter. A simple but illuminating exercise is to tabulate from the censuses the population of seaside resorts at different times and set them against the dates of railway construction. Directories and guidebooks can then be used to list hotels and boarding houses, and there are likely to be photographs and descriptions illustrating the attractions of the place.

As with earlier periods, contemporary travellers' and observers' accounts are also useful. Daniel Defoe's descriptions contain a great deal of information on trade and industry, including markets and fairs and the organization of the textile industries on the eve of industrialization (though sometimes his chronology is a little suspect). His account of the West Riding cloth industry before the factory era is a well-known example of his analytical writing. Such works can be used with older children not only for comprehensive exercises but as a lead into a more detailed examination of local industry generally. They form excellent material for the stimulation of imaginative work—such as 'diaries', stories, 'letters', playlets, 'eye-witness' and 'newspaper' accounts. Sometimes there will be historical novels which can add insight to the purely historical evidence. For the West Riding in this period, for example, there is Phyllis Bentley's *Gold Pieces* (1968). Other contemporary accounts will provide material for different sorts of activity. Keeping to the West Riding woollen industry as an example, the following account of 1795, while less colourful and detailed than Defoe's, could lead to a good deal of map work and an investigation of different types of cloth manufactured.[11]

The whole number of master broad-cloth manufacturers in the West Riding of Yorkshire is about 3,240. The mixed cloth manufacturers reside partly in the villages belonging to the parish of Leeds; but chiefly at Morley, Guildersome, Adwalton, Driglington, Pudsey, Farsley, Calverley, Eccleshall, Idle, Baildon, Yeadon, Guisely, Rawdon, and Horsforth, in or bordering upon the vale of Aire, chiefly west of Leeds; and at Batley, Dewsbury, Ossett, Horbury, and Kirkburton, west of Wakefield, in or near the vale of Calder. Not a single manufacturer is to be found more than one mile east, or two north, of Leeds; nor are there many in the town of Leeds, and those only in the outskirts.

The white cloth is manufactured chiefly at Alverthorpe, Ossett, Kirkheaton, Dewsbury, Batley, Birstal, Hopton, Mirfield, Archet, Clackheaton, Littletown, Bowling, and Shipley ... The districts of the white and coloured cloth manufactory are generally distinct, but are a little intermixed at the south-east and north-west extremities. The cloths are sold in their respective halls rough as they come from the fulling mills. They are finished by the merchants, who employ dressers, dyers, &c., for that purpose; these, with drysalters, shopkeepers, and

the different kind of handicraftsmen common to every town, compose
the bulk of the inhabitants of Leeds . . .

For local industry in the nineteenth century the published parliamentary papers (or 'Blue Books') are perhaps the most fruitful single
source for teaching purposes, for many of the major industries of the
century were the subject of official investigation. Good descriptions of
the factory districts from the early nineteenth century are to be found
in reports concerned with the employment of women and children
and in the annual factory and mine inspectors' reports. Edited collections of these have too often overstressed the textile districts, but
teachers will find reports just as interesting and vital for other
industries – such as the potteries and other Midland trades, where
domestic production often continued to flourish in an atmosphere of
even greater degradation than in the factory towns. There is plenty of
material on the conditions of domestic textile workers in districts
where hand-loom weaving and framework knitting maintained a
twilight survival. Reports on the poor law, public health, aspects of
housing, sanitation, water supply, scientific and technical education,
transport and communications, and so on, also contain details of
industry and trade in different localities. The sweating industries,
the truck system, the trade unions are all treated in parliamentary
papers at various times, and the official indexes and W. R. Powell's
Local History from Blue Books should be searched. All these reports
cannot be illustrated here, but a few may be mentioned to give an
idea of the wealth of variety they contain. The report of 1816 on
child labour in factories contains, for example, Josiah Wedgwood's
own evidence on the child labour at Etruria. There children of eleven
to fourteen years worked for thirteen and a half hours a day, exclusive
of meal times, attending the dippers, cleaning and brushing the ware
and removing it after it was dipped and dried. It is often easier for
pupils to perform the feat of imagining themselves in the place of
children than of adults in the past. For that reason evidence like this
is particularly helpful for stimulating imaginative and pictorial work
of all kinds. The evidence of parents, children, employers and others
before official committees lends itself particularly to dramatic activities, for an almost ready-made script is often there. Straight playlets,
edited by the children, are suitable both for juniors and younger
secondary-school pupils. Older pupils may attempt, too, tape-recorded
dialect plays or documentaries on such themes as 'social conditions
in our county in the factory age'. Such an extract as the following

testimony from the 1840s of a Scots girl from Edmonstone colliery in Newton could form the basis of an imaginative exercise or as a stimulus to investigation of child conditions in the mines in the area. (*First Report of the Children's Employment Commission*, 1842).

> Isabella Read, 11 years old, coal bearer: I have been below at the coal work 12 months or more. I gang at four or five in the morning and come up at three or four at night and later. I can fill a tub of 4½ cwt in four journeys; a journey is nearly half a mile back and forward. I can fill four and sometimes five tubs a day now.
>
> I have not been at school since down; was at Miss Hunters' school, she taught me to read and sew; has been to Sabbath-school; thinks that there are six commandments; can't recollect the questions. I am away from work, as I injured my knee. [Reads very badly.]

In places which took no part in the industrial revolution a proper question a teacher might pose to a class of older children is why this was so. The work involved in discovering the answer can be most stimulating and may result not only in insight into the factors involved in early industrialization but into the effect of general industrial growth on areas where such activity was not to be found.

For the later nineteenth and early twentieth centuries local chambers of commerce sometimes published occasional booklets describing local industries and giving details of local firms—including their history, their products, the processes they used, their marketing activities and the size and nature of their labour force. These, like directories and local newspapers and periodicals, often contain informative advertisements. Where these take the form of pictorial representations of goods or factories they can be fascinating to children of all ages and often add greatly to their understanding. Local newspapers are, of course, a mine of information on all aspects of town life, including industry and trade. They do, however, require preliminary searching by the teacher. This can be tedious and time-consuming, but it is essential. While it may be useful to show children whole newspapers, they cannot normally be set to search through them for suitable information. The teacher must make his own series of extracts for reproduction for class use. In some cases he will find that libraries, or local newspaper offices, have indexes to past copies. Sometimes librarians or others have compiled books of cuttings arranged by topics.

For the Victorian period and later, published histories of important firms often exist. Usually such firms will be only too pleased to present copies to schools, but usually there will be copies in local libraries. As well as providing straight accounts of the history of the firms and the local industries of which they were part, valuable primary source material is often reproduced in these works. Some original business records, of course, may be available in local record offices and libraries, or with the firms themselves. These can include wages books, inventories of stock, prospectuses, trade circulars and copies of correspondence—all of which may be useful in the classroom if copied.

Children living in ports may have a special interest in sea-going trade in modern, as earlier, times. Maps and plans (as discussed in the last chapter) can be used for the study of the growth or decline of dock and harbour facilities, and local newspapers will shed light on shipping movements and the nature of trade. For the eighteenth century the port books (described above) may still be of use. In addition shipbuilders' records, bills of sale, cargo books, log books, and records of ship owners' mutual insurance clubs are all types of source material suitable for teachers' purposes which may exist in local record offices. At the Cornwall County Record Office, for example, there is an account book of a schooner which includes details of the cost of construction and the financial accounts for twelve voyages. Registers of local shipping from 1786 exist at the customs houses of certain ports. These provide the name of each vessel, its place and year of construction, details of ownership, descriptive details (including number of decks and masts, rig, type of build) dimensions (including size of hold, height between decks) and tonnage. If the vessel has ceased to exist its final fate is noted.[12] Such information is best used in conjunction with books of reference, museum models and photographs, which are likely to exist in most port towns. For some places, especially fishing ports, certain parliamentary papers are of value. There are, for example, reports on the fisheries of south Devon in 1817, on the Bristol Channel fisheries in 1833, and on sea fisheries in 1866, which contain much fascinating information.

Children, especially boys, brought up in ports may well have a particular interest in ships and the sea, and if the teacher himself is an expert in such matters or can call on expert advice, class work of a project type can prove most rewarding.[13] All sorts of practical activity can be undertaken with children of different ages. For types of ships modelling, photographs and pictorial representation can all be used. Map and model work can deal with the history of harbours and docks. Those pupils with a technical bent can compile booklets and wall diagrams to explain the types of ships, how they were constructed, how they were powered, and so on. For others the social side of the life of sailors and their families can be investigated. The trade of the port, the routes used, and the goods dealt in, can also be studied, maps made, and perhaps imaginative work based on ships' logs, registers and other material undertaken. In this way the purely local history of the port can be used to lead into more general national or extra-national history.

Farming from Tudor times

Agricultural history is a topic where regional differences are particularly evident. Although most parts of the country in early modern and more recent times have shared in general advancement, change was greater in some places than others at certain times. Periods of depression and prosperity were not necessarily nation-wide experiences: for always the type of farming has to be taken into account. For Tudor and Stuart times a clue to the nature of local farming organization may be obtained from glebe terriers, of which many exist.[14] These were descriptions of the parson's dwelling and land, and they provide good teaching material. From them may be deduced not only valuable information on local topography but also, for example, the spread of enclosure. If the terrier shows that the glebe land was distributed in strips over a number of large fields, this will be clear evidence that open-field strip farming was still being practised in that village. If the parson's land is recorded as being concentrated in blocks within several fields it is likely that other villagers also had consolidated holdings probably formed by the exchange of strips. If the parson had land in hedged enclosures, then it may be that more general enclosure had taken place in the village, although there is the possibility that the church land was an exception. Sometimes a terrier will specifically record an enclosure agreement and perhaps describe the glebe holding both before and after enclosure. Some terriers have been published, many others are to be found in diocesan and other local record offices or with parish records.

Though many glebe terriers are fairly easy to read, they are difficult for most children to use without assistance. Nevertheless they remain excellent for illustrative purposes with the teacher indicating the information they can yield. For example, from the terrier of Burford in 1501, of which the following is a brief extract,[15] it can be seen that the rector's lands were scattered among those of other tenants and that the fields were therefore not yet enclosed. With guidance older children, looking at the whole terrier in conjunction with OS and other maps, can tentatively reconstruct the topography and field pattern of the parish

Bampton waye furlong.
Item in a furlonge that goeth over Bampeton waye iii acres whereof di. acre lyethe betwene the churche lands of Burforde on the est and the land called Heystonysland on the west and one lyethe betwene the land of Thomas Pole one bothe syde est and west and di. unius acre abbuttethe upon the northe ende of the same Acar towarde the northe and lyethe betwene the lande of William Pattern of Synete on the west and the lands of the churche of Burford on the est . . .

Westerhen furlonge.
Item in Westerhenfurlong di. an acre which lyeth betwene the land of Wm fflydygate north & the church land south.

The sort of sources which may be used to illustrate enclosure for sheep in the Tudor period and for later parliamentary enclosure are discussed in Chapter 6. For the eighteenth and nineteenth centuries there are a number of interesting sources giving detailed information on local agriculture. The *General Views of Agriculture* were descriptions sponsored by the Board of Agriculture and published in a series of county volumes. Usually there is a first edition published in the 1790s and a second, updated edition in the early nineteenth century.[16] Some have been reprinted recently and should thus be easy to obtain. By comparing the two editions some indication may be ascertained of changes at a time when the pressures of the French wars and the efforts of the advocates of 'agricultural revolution' were securing advances in farming methods and organization. Such a task would, however, be best confined to sixth- or academically inclined fifth-formers. There are plenty of other uses to which these reports can be put, too. For older pupils generally they can provide both exercises and illustrative material. Younger children will be able to use suitably edited extracts for the purposes of imaginative exercises, or for compiling information about various aspects of farming and farm life at the time. The following extract from the *General View* for the West Riding (1794) provides, for example, an illustration of the farm wage structure in the vale of Skipton and the effect of alternative factory work on it—again a useful antidote to the conceptions of the industrial revolution as totally injurious to working people.

Price of labour. A man servant about ten guineas per year, with board and washing in his master's house; a woman about five guineas, with the same; day labourers in husbandry about 2*s* or 2*s* 6*d* per day, finding their own victuals: about ten years ago, 1*s* or 1*s* 2*d* was the common price; the advance owing to the introduction of the cotton manufactory into a country so little populous. They work from six to six in summer, and from eight to dark in winter.

The writings of Arthur Young, whose name will usually be found in school textbooks for the period, will also often be useful. Again these are not difficult to obtain, and the following extract—a letter to Young from a Leicestershire clergyman—is an indication of their value:[17]

Taking a fair view upon the whole, both before, and since the enclosure, there is more grain since the enclosure brought to market; a greater produce from sheep and young cattle, and considerably more than double the quantity of cheese made in the parish. A great deal of waste land, &c before the enclosure, the produce of which was but trifling, is now drained, and with proper cultivation, is become the finest land, and the greatest crops are got therefrom. . . .

Attractive sources for class use for the early Victorian period include tithe commutation maps and schedules, which have been described fully in the last chapter. For the period of 'high farming' between the repeal of the corn laws and the agricultural depression of the latter decades of the century another set of county descriptions was published as prize essays in issues of the *Journal of the Royal Agricultural Society*.[18] These can provide not only detailed local information but also for older pupils a valuable comparison with the earlier descriptions in the *General Views*. Parliamentary papers also provide good teaching material for agriculture and rural life.[19] Reports on the depressed state of farming after the Napoleonic wars and into the 1830s and similar reports on the depression in the latter decades of the century are full of good illustrative material for different parts of the country. So, too, are reports on female and child labour: a report of 1843, for example, covers twelve counties (Wiltshire, Dorset, Devon, Somerset, Kent, Surrey, Sussex, Suffolk, Norfolk, Lincolnshire, Yorkshire and Northumberland) and another published in several volumes between 1868 and 1870 covers many counties. The following extract, from the report of 1843, is an indication of human material which children of the middle and secondary-school age groups find captivating:

Charles Medway, of Doddiscombleigh, Devonshire, Farm-labourer, examined.

I was born at Bridford. My father and mother were farmers' labourers. I am 39 years old. I was apprenticed to Mr. Smallridge, of Bridford, a farmer: he had a farm of 230 acres. I was first put out at six years old to a place to fetch cows, water, &c. I was afterwards, between seven and eight, apprenticed. My master died one year before my time was out; I served the rest out with his widow. There were three or four other apprentices at the same time; two of them girls. It was a very good place, as good a place as a person could wish to be in: plenty of meat and drink. As for work, why people must work, and there was plenty of that. The boys lodged with master's sons, in the same room; the girls slept in another room with master's daughters. There were 21 of us in the family all at one time. I was clothed pretty well: I had two suits, one for Sunday and one for week days. I always went decent to any place on a holiday. There was never any serious disagreements between master and mistress and their apprentices; a few words, perhaps, but none of them ever went before a magistrate. I was living much better in the farm-house than I might be at home.

I married at 28. I have got four children; the eldest is a boy of 10. He lives in a farm-house; he works for his meat, drink, and clothes and lodging, but he is not apprenticed.

I think it is good thing for boys to be apprenticed. They used to be beat sometimes where I was; a stick or whip was used. We didn't like it, but now I think it was necessary. Where there are several young people together they must be done so to keep them in order ... I learned to read in the farm-house. Master took care we should read of winter nights, on Sundays particularly. All the apprentices were brought to the reading in the same way. I went to church twice on Sunday generally. I said my catechism every Sunday to my master; he made his sons and daughters attend to us. I was confirmed: master was always anxious about that with his apprentices ... but I was lucky. I know many places where I should not like a child to be sent to ... but, generally speaking, places are good.

Often local record offices will also contain estate and farm records for the modern period. These may include maps, wage books, herd and flock books, diaries and memoranda, and other miscellaneous information. Sale catalogues for farms and estates are also attractive and useful sources for class use. There is a large collection of farm and estate records at the University of Reading library, which periodically issues up-to-date catalogues, but many county record offices will have some of this type of material.

Often the most valuable way to use the sources discussed above is in a class project, for clearly they should for any particular area be used in combination. Thus tithe maps, as well as being used for topographical work, can form the basis, together with the tithe schedules, for a large-scale class exercise. Groups of secondary-school pupils can, for example, produce an analysis of the pattern of land ownership and its relation to tenant holding. Copies of the map can be used to plot areas owned by different landowners, to indicate how many were owner-occupiers, or what areas were farmed by tenants. Other maps can be produced showing how the land was used. If other information is available, as from literary descriptions or such sources as the *General Views*, it may be possible for older children to build up a changing picture of land use and crops grown in a locality over a period. Teachers whose work is oriented to social or environmental studies can then get their pupils to carry out a comparison with present-day land use in the district, and to find out what contemporary farmers are growing.

Work of this kind should if possible include fieldwork (see Chapter 8). This will not only reveal the nature of present-day farming but also show how far ancient field boundaries, or changes made at the time of enclosure, are still evident in one way or another, and to what extent later developments have been affected by them. Studies of farmhouses and outbuildings, as well as farm cottages, can also be undertaken on the ground, augmented by photographic sources where available, and the evidence from such parliamentary papers as indicated above can bring to life the attitudes and experiences of farmers, labourers and others who lived in rural areas at different periods. These and the other of the types of record discussed above can lead to imaginative work, written and oral, to descriptive accounts and the making of graphs and tables.

Population and social structure
The social and demographic structure of local, especially urban, communities in the medieval and early modern periods has already proved a fruitful and popular area for school history. The chief sources are religious and tax records. Domesday is discussed in Chapter 6. Fourteenth-century poll tax records, especially those for 1379 are a medieval source of some use for estimates of total population and the spread of wealth, though if they have not been published by a local record society it is doubtful whether it is worth while obtaining copies from the Public Record Office.[20] The seventeenth century often provides demographic sources particularly useful for

classroom work. If they exist for the place concerned, poll tax returns, hearth tax returns and probate inventories, used in conjunction, can bring to life most vividly the nature of the social structure of local communities. Sometimes poll and hearth tax returns will be available in print, but where they are not there may be originals in the local record office or the Public Record Office. Then the purchase of copies would be well worth while, for the documents are usually reasonably easy to read. The poll tax returns will show the amounts paid by each adult (or married couple). The tax was graded by rank in the case of 'gentlemen' and above and clergy, and by income for others, with youths and humblest folk paying a flat rate of sixpence or a shilling. Paupers and those under sixteen were exempt and not usually recorded. By simple calculations pupils can tabulate or make block graphs of the numbers paying at different rates, so revealing the structure of prosperity. If the following return for the parish of St Pancras, Exeter, in 1660,[21] for example, is so analysed it will show forty-four individuals or couples paying the minimum flat rate (1*s*) out of a total of sixty-seven individual or paired payers. Perhaps half a dozen of the forty-four were youngsters living with parents, yet the broad base of the social pyramid is demonstrated, and the teacher can point out that below this were those exempt on grounds of poverty.

PARISH OF ST PANCRAS

John Mongwell
Thomas Atherton   Collectors

Elizabeth Flay, widow	£4 0*s* 0*d*
Richard Simmons	12*d*
Philip Slocombe	12*d*
Margaret Easton	12*d*
Amy Filley	12*d*
Edward Foxwell & wife	£4 0*s* 6*d*
Margaret Burrington	12*s*
Margaret Foxwell	12*d*
Ellianor Williams	12*d*
Robert Taylor	12*d*
Anne Foxwell	12*d*
Philippa Summers, widow	5*s*
Thomas Savory & wife	10*s* 6*d*
Margaret Severicke	12*d*
Francis Sanders	12*d*
Grace Parr	4*s*

Susanna Parr	4*s*
Anne Parr	4*s*
Mary Foxwell, widow	5*s*
John Foxwell & wife	10*s* 6*d*
George Foxwell	12*d*
Anne Bickford	12*d*
Elizabeth Clatworthy	12*d*
Benjamin Beard & wife	7*s* 6*d*
Richard North	2*s* 6*d*
John Wills	12*d*
Peter Battishill	12*d*
John Rowcliffe	12*d*
Alice Martyn	5*s*
Edward Copleston	2*s*
Elizabeth Copleston	12*d*
Mary Prideaux, widow	£3 6*s* 8*d*
Dorothy Southard	12*d*
John Robins & wife	5*s* 6*d*
Mary Robins	12*d*
John Mongwell & wife	15*s*
John Passmore	12*d*
Edward Portbury	12*d*
John Mountstephen	12*d*
Thomas Atherton & wife	20*s* 6*d*
John Palmer	12*d*
Joan Coleman	12*d*
Giles Burchyoung	12*d*
Peter Taylor & wife	15*s* 6*d*
John Hayman	12*d*
Anne Holsworth	12*d*
Agnes Upton	12*d*
Peter Turner & wife	10*s* 6*d*
John Turner	12*d*
Susanna Turner	12*d*
Thomas Dix & wife	15*s* 6*d*
Susanna Gregory	2*s*
Thomas Dix, jun.	12*d*
John Brenly	12*d*
Thomas Macumber	12*d*
Anne Syms	12*d*
Edward Wood & wife	5*s* 6*d*
Zacheus Lee	12*d*
Elizabeth Wall	12*d*
Margery White	12*d*

George Rogers & wife	12*d*
Michael Mill	12*d*
Richard Evans & wife	12*d*
Honor Widwell, widow	12*d*
Thomas Somerton & wife	12*d*
William Somerton & wife	12*d*
Thomas Scorch & wife	12*d*
Total	£21 13*s* 8*d*

The returns for the hearth tax (levied from 1662) are also arranged by parishes, with the number of hearths or stoves (not money amounts) against each householder. Junior children can use these to make diagrams showing how many houses of different sizes there were in the parish—seven three-hearth houses, twenty four-hearth houses, and so on. The teacher should point out, however, that sometimes a large number of hearths for one building indicates an inn rather than a private dwelling. Older children can carry out similar analytical exercises and also attempt, from both poll and hearth tax returns, to make estimates of the total population at different times. Thus in poll tax returns a rough ratio of recorded adult payers to unrecorded children of six to four may be assumed. From this a total can be deduced which will not, however, include paupers—who perhaps accounted for 15–20 per cent of the total population. Hearth tax records sometimes list those exempted as well as those who paid, but the payers here are householders only. Here a multiplier of four to five per householder can be applied, and to the result can be added the number of exempted persons—usually aged paupers, often living alone. Thus a rough estimate of total population can again be obtained.

With older pupils, and where a teacher has investigated the sources well, it is possible to undertake more enterprising projects. Poll and hearth taxes were both levied in the post-Restoration period and often records of both are available for the same place for years not too far apart. Population estimates calculated from each source can obviously be compared with advantage in such cases. A more detailed analysis of the social structure of the community is also possible. Since the returns of both types of tax name the payers, some of the same persons may be identified in each. In such cases an indication will be seen of the relationship between the size of a person's house (from the number of hearths) and certain levels of poll tax. Tentative definition of social groupings can then be attempted.

Other records can be used to help identify important personages. In towns borough and gild records (Chapter 6) will provide the names of the richer inhabitants who were mayors or held other civic or gild offices. If probate inventories are available the community may really be brought to life.[22] Such inventories name the deceased and list, room by room, his household belongings. They note also ready money and money owed and owing, together with a valuation of all the chattels. Inventories are attractive documents which for the seventeenth century children can learn to read fairly easily. If the teacher can provide copies of inventories for a number of the persons listed in the poll and hearth tax returns it is possible, for example, to write a full description of the five hearth house of John Smith, yeoman, who paid over £5 in the poll. If one or two persons from each tax category can be identified the material conditions of people in different local social strata can be illustrated. Since the inventories also indicate the trade or profession of the deceased, the comparative wealth of different types of tradesmen can also be indicated. Even if only one or other of a hearth or poll tax return is available, with the aid of inventories and other contemporary evidence to identify some people a very interesting exercise is possible.

The local librarian or archivist will be able to indicate the availability of these tax records and inventories. Teachers of children below the age of, say, fourteen, may well find that such exercises as those just described are too ambitious. They will certainly, however, find that inventories are useful in their own right. They exist in large numbers in local record offices in manuscript, and being not too difficult to read are favourites with junior and middle school pupils. Some have appeared in print. The teacher will find numerous ways in which they can be utilized. They can, for example, illustrate how rural some towns were in the early modern period, with farming activities in evidence, or they can provide details of the tools and stock of craftsmen. The following for a baker in 1642 will act as an example:[23]

PHILLIP STEVENS of Crediton, Whitebaker. By John Rowe and William Coles, 2 August 1642

All his lyninen and wollen Aparrell £6 13s 4d; His Plate £24; His Bookes 13s; His Pewter and tyning Commiodityes £2 16s; One high Press 2 high bedstedes with matteres and Coardes belonging to them £3 10s; 2 ioynt stooles, one table board one forme and a piece of seeling IN THE FORECHAMBER £1 5s; One Coffer one Cupbord cloth & Cushion 7s; His sheetes table napkins table clothes Pillowties etc £2 2s; One feather bed three bolsters one dust bed 4 ruges and 2 Curtaynes £7; One Board one boxe IN THE MIDLE CHAMBER 8s; One halfeheaded bedstead with a duste bed a Courelett and blankett £1;

Wicker vesselles 1s 6d; 10 Bushelles of meale £3 6s 8d; His Brass Pottes brass Pannes and other utensilles of Brass £7; All his yron stuffe or utensilles of yron £1; One Limbicke 6s; One old settle and a Racke IN THE YEILDING HOUSE 2s;

IN THE BREWHOUSE: Moulding Bordes brewing keiues and other timber utensilles therto belonging and other timber vesselles in other outehouses £2 10s; 11 Bagges, rangers & one howerglass 9s; IN TWO OUTROOMES: Two table bordes & 2 formes 10s; IN THE CELLAR: 2 hogsheades of Beere with 2 hogsheades and other ymplementes therein £3 6s 8d; IN THE BRADHOUSE: The bread Cups Jugges and other things 5s;

IN THE HALL: One Jacke & waightes 10s; In the Spence in the hall: One hatchett one ring bittle & other thinges there 1s 6d; In the hall: One table borde, Seeling the Spence there & other thinges £2 5s; 2 goosepans one pessell & morter & plate Cullender some ordinarye candlestickes & some other smale thinges 8s;

His provision of Sope Candles salte groates and fishe 5s; Trenchers tynninge Spoones wooden dishes and earthen vessells 5s; His woode, ladder Reede and other thinges £1; 10 swyen hoges troughs & dounge £6 13s 4d; His Bakon 3s 4d; In readie money 17s.

Total   £80 19s 4d

Exhibited by Ann the widow 21 December 1642

Inventories thus provide teaching materials for pupils of all ages. Much work with dictionaries and works of reference will be needed to identify all the objects listed, and here the *Oxford English Dictionary* is invaluable. A glossary can then be compiled; plans or pictorial representations of rooms can be made; wall friezes, models and pictures of houses and their contents can be prepared; and comparison of the contents of present-day rooms with their Tudor or Stuart equivalents can be drawn up. Above all, the inventory can form the basis of imaginative writing. Where craftsmen's tools and stock are included lists can be made and visits to local museums and libraries made to identify them, and comparison with modern shops and factories undertaken.

There will be scope for team work or class projects. One child or group could be sent to find out more about the types of furniture mentioned in a number of local inventories; others about kitchen utensils, household goods, clothing, and tools and stock for various trades. Other children could attempt to relate the description of the rooms to contemporary information on national or local housing. What, for example, was a buttery, a solar, a parlour? And so on. Sometimes a surviving house of the period can be found in the locality and visited.

Another early modern source is the Protestation Returns of 1642. At that time the Commons required all men of eighteen and over to sign a declaration 'protesting' their support for Parliament. The returns consist of lists of signatures (and names of those who refused or were unable to sign). For many parishes, therefore, we have a list of the total adult male population. The originals are at the House of Lords Record Office, and copies may be purchased.[24] A rough indication of the population of a place can be obtained by assuming that there was an equal number of women as men, and that 40 per cent of the population were children. A good exercise is to carry out such a calculation for a number of places in the locality of the school to provide a comparison of the size of population. This can be repeated for 1676 by using the Compton census returns, which provide by parishes the number of Anglican communicants, Protestant dissenters and Roman Catholics over the age of about sixteen. Many of these are at Lambeth Palace and the William Salt Library, Stafford, and copies should be sought. For the seventeenth and eighteenth centuries bishops' visitation returns (Chapter 7) give similar information for many places at different times. Such records can, of course, be used also as a lead into, or as part of, a study of religious and political division, local and national.

Parish registers are a source known to most laymen, and their value to the professional historical demographer has been enhanced in recent years by the refinement of analytical practices. The technique of 'family reconstruction' has been developed and more sophisticated methods of 'aggregative' analysis have been devised. Since D. Turner's *Historical Demography in Schools* (Hist. Assoc., 1971) is largely devoted to an explanation of these methods, with suggestions for their use, I do not intend to dwell on them here. On the whole I feel that work of this kind with parish registers is more appropriate to adult classes than to schools. The new techniques are time-consuming and difficult even for sixth-formers, and for pupils of all ages the time involved in counting and calculating could be better spent. Some elementary exercises involving parish registers can, however, be usefully devised for older juniors and upwards. Numbers of baptisms, deaths and marriages over a period can be graphed; the reasons for deaths tabulated (see fig. 1); ages at death and the number of infant

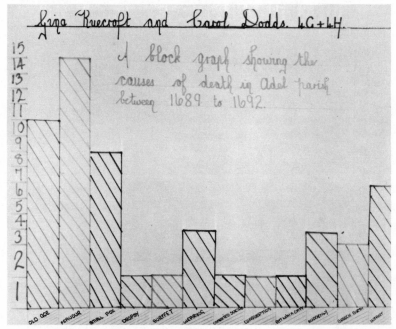

1   An example of the work of children on parish registers

deaths can be calculated (see fig. 2). Such studies can lead into further
work in general or local history, as, for example, the history of public
health and housing, and medicine. Occasionally it will be possible to
demonstrate from a burial register the effects of an epidemic on a community. Evidence on the movement of population can be found in
marriage registers, and the findings can be analysed or plotted on
maps to show how many of those married came from outside the
parish and from what places.

Original registers may still be in the incumbent's care or deposited
in a local record office. In a large number of cases they have been
published. A new series, the *National Index of Parish Registers* (in
progress), will list in a dozen topographically arranged volumes not
only Anglican but Roman Catholic and Nonconformist registers and
before long will provide an invaluable finding aid. The original
enumerators' books for the 1841, 1851, 1861 and 1871 censuses (the
equivalent of the modern returns made by householders for the
census) can be used to repopulate in the pupils' imagination whole

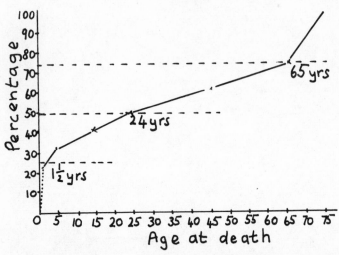

THE AVERAGE AGE OF MALE DEATHS.
1841 — 1870

2   An example of a junior-school boy's work on parish registers

streets. These reveal the sort of people who lived in each street—their homes, occupations, the numbers and ages of members of each family, numbers and personal details of servants, the number of children at school (shown as 'scholar') and their ages, information on migration (from 1851 places of birth are shown) and more besides. A detailed reconstruction of the social and occupational structure of a street or a small area, using not only census material but also maps and directories, can be undertaken and can provide the basis for numerous class projects on local or general topics concerned with Victorian social life.[25] There is much scope, too, for individual work such as tables, block graphs, descriptions and so on. It may be that the street still exists, and a study of the present-day inhabitants can be undertaken for comparative purposes—especially where local or environmental studies are being taught. The original enumerators' books are at the Public Record Office, but copies may be purchased from there and some local libraries have already obtained microfilm of those for their own area. The following (edited) example of an enumerators' return (for part of Dover Street, Folkestone, 1871) gives an indication of the sort of information provided.

It must be remembered, however, that the enumerators' books were

Name	Relation to head of family	Condition	Age M	Age F	Occupation	Where born
Edward Baker	Head	Mar.	51		House painter	Folkestone
Elizabeth *do.*	Wife	,,		50		,,
Joseph Howlett	Head	,,	59		Schoolmaster	Gt. Yarmouth
Mary *do.*	Wife	,,		45	Schoolmistress	Folkestone
Susanna Lepper	Head	Wid.		39	Charwoman	,,
John *do.*	Son	Unm.	17		Carpenter	,,
Thomas M. *do.*	,,	,,	6			Sheerness
Thomas Nash	Head	Mar.	52		Shoemaker	Folkestone
Mary *do.*	Wife	,,		53		,,
John *do.*	Son	–	15		Scholar	,,
Margaret *do.*	Dau.	Unm.		18	Domestic Servant	,,
Mary *do.*	,,	,,		17	,, ,,	,,

the basis for the published census reports, which contain for all parts of the country extremely detailed statistical information, particularly on occupations and the distribution of population. Moreover these reports exist for all the census years and not merely for 1841–71, and local reference libraries will certainly have appropriate volumes. There has been a tendency to forget the existence of these parliamentary papers and to allow attention to be monopolized by the enumerators' books, when the printed volumes can yield so much. These are particularly useful for group work with older children and if the teacher can provide copies of relevant sections for a number of censuses, much good comparative work can be undertaken. Graphs of the total populations of local towns and villages over the period 1801 to 1971 can be made, as well as tables or diagrams of age and sex distribution in various census years. The changing occupational structure can be indicated in written descriptions or diagramatic form, making use, too, of other sources for occupations and industries. As one nears the present day history of this kind merges with social studies, so that census studies may well be appropriate to school leavers' classes.

For notes to this chapter see pp. 168–9.

6 Local history to illustrate national history: I

Although national and general history may be taught adequately with little reference to local history, teachers have long found that for certain topics the use of local examples often adds both insight and interest. Of course, source material can be used which is not local, but where appropriate a local document is usually to be preferred, for it helps to destroy the remoteness and strangeness of much national history.

Some aspects of national history, especially wars, diplomacy and much domestic political history, do not usually lend themselves to local exemplification. On the other hand so many topics can be illustrated at the local level that it would be impossible to treat them all here. I have, therefore, concentrated on a few topics, to provide detailed examples. It should be noted, however, that many of the topics covered in the previous two chapters as suitable for local history in its own right can often be used, too, to illustrate those themes nationally. Chapters 4 and 5 should, therefore, be referred to even by teachers who do not intend to deal with purely local history, especially for such topics as communications, population and social structure, industry, trade and agriculture. In this and the next chapter I discuss in some detail aspects of political, religious, economic and social history often taught as part of general history syllabuses. Some of these will, of course, also be of use to those teaching social and environmental studies.

Farming and rural life in the Middle Ages
It is unlikely that sufficient source material of the kind suitable for children will exist for the study of medieval local rural society in its own right. It is very probable, however, that there will be enough to put flesh on the bare bones of the usual general treatment of the topic and to give some insight into the nature of the local community at the same time. Medieval records in accessible form are, however, considerably fewer than those that exist for more recent times, and

the teacher may well have to use some relating to a number of different places over a comparatively wide local area to illustrate his themes. Since what is familiarly local to the informed adult may be as remote as China, and remoter than the holiday beaches of Spain, to many children, even though perhaps only a few miles distant from the school, pupils should be taken to see the places concerned as they exist today, to be shown any physical remains or topographical peculiarities surviving from the past, and to mark them clearly on maps. A larger map kept on the wall of the classroom for the period of the study is also essential.

Sources which can be used to illustrate at a local level the social structure of rural communities and manorial life in the Middle Ages include Domesday, custumals, rentals, extents or surveys, manorial court rolls and manorial accounts. If the Middle Ages is taken as lasting from Anglo-Saxon times to the end of the fifteenth century it is likely that a number of such records will be available in print, hopefully some in translation, for most parts of the country. Where they have been reproduced in the original Latin the teacher must not be too easily deterred from using them.[1] They are often in a form of Latin not very difficult to translate, but if this proves too great a barrier then the assistance of a local archivist, Latin teacher or other specialist will be worth seeking.

Local entries in the Domesday Book used in conjunction with the Anglo-Saxon chronicles, the Bayeux tapestry and some of the types of records described below can form the basis for a 'patch' study of the Norman conquest and of medieval England generally. For most places Domesday will also provide the first description of local communities, and in particular their feudal structure and farming resources. Although Domesday was published in record type in 1783 most teachers will find it essential to obtain a modern translation. The translations published county by county in the *Victoria County History* are usually available in local libraries, and a new translation with facsimiles is currently being produced by Phillimore's. Considering the usefulness of Domesday for teaching, some detailed comments may be useful. Entries within each county are arranged by landholders, so that some places, if they fell within the bounds of more than one manor, may have more than one entry. It is essential, therefore, to use the *V.C.H.* index carefully. The information given in the various entries may differ somewhat, but usually an entry includes the name of the holder at the time of the conquest, the names of the overlord and under-tenant in 1086, and the number of peasant heads of families and other individuals. Thus the entry for Dewsbury (Yorkshire), which states that there were six villeins, two bordars and a priest, may be taken to mean that apart from the priest the population consisted of eight villein families. Historians usually assume a family size of about four or five for this period, so that some thirty to forty peasants probably lived at Dewsbury then.

Each entry usually provides, too, an estimate of the value of the manor at the time of the survey and at the Conquest, twenty years before. In some parts of the country the disastrous effects of military operations are evidenced by the indication that once valuable holdings were by 1086 'waste'. This was so notably in the north of England, but also in some other places. Beeston (Bedfordshire), for example, was unvalued in 1086, though it had been worth 20*s* in 1066. Then there will usually be evidence on land use. Details will often be given of the amount of meadow, pasture and woodland (and some-times forest) in each manor, the number of existing plough (teams) (distinguishing those on the demesne and those of the peasantry) and perhaps how many plough teams would be needed to work the land fully. A mill may also be mentioned. Pasture land was given some-times in acres or very frequently in linear measures of leagues and furlongs, which may be difficult to turn into modern acreages. Thus the manor of Otley (Yorkshire) had pasturable woodland of '2 leagues and 3 furlongs in length and as much in breadth'. Often the amount of woodland was expressed in the number of swine it could support— so that in Middlesex Dawley's Woods could feed fifteen while other manors ranged upwards from that to 2,000 each at Harrow, Edmon-ton and Enfield. In some places marshes, moors and salt pans were mentioned, and occasionally vineyards (as at Stonehouse, Glouces-tershire, and Chart Sutton, Kent) and beehives (as at Saffron Walden). Markets for agricultural produce are noted here and there, as at Tewkesbury, and very occasionally a fair, as at Eye (Suffolk).

The second volume of Domesday, covering Essex, Norfolk and Suffolk, and the Exon Domesday, devoted to the counties of the south-west, record details of the livestock held on each demesne. Thus as at Theydon in Ongar (Essex) the entry comparing stock in 1066 and 1086 runs 'Then as now 2 rounceys. Then 8 animals, now 13. Then 35 swine, now 66. Then 87 sheep, now 100 and 15 goats.'

Before attempting to make use of the Domesday entries for his area in the classroom the teacher should read carefully the relevant section in the volumes of regional Domesday studies written by H. C. Darby and his collaborators.[2] These analyse county by county the sorts of information to be obtained from the Domesday entries for each county, with particular reference to common attributes of settlements, and give advice on the interpretation of entries, with many specific examples. Every school library should try to obtain the volume covering its area.

In the classroom Domesday can be used in many ways as well as the purely illustrative. Exercises can include the plotting on maps of local places mentioned in the survey, using symbols to indicate mention of churches, mills, fishponds and so on. Estimates of their population can be made and tabulated, and these compared with the population at later dates (see Chapter 5). Older children can see similarly how the places compare in the extent of meadow, pasture and so on, and the values of each place in 1066 and 1086 can also be compared, perhaps expressing their findings in tables or pie diagrams. Upper juniors and older children can also analyse the numbers in each feudal group and see if they vary greatly from place to place locally, and these calculations can also be translated into tables and diagrams. With help from the teacher, who can contribute his knowledge of local historical topography, it is possible for pupils to draw a tentative plan of a Domesday manor and then make it into a relief model. Not all Domesday entries, however, are sufficiently full to lend themselves to this.

Other exercises can be devised to illustrate the feudal structure of England from the local communities. Maps can be constructed to show the holdings of different landowners in an area. Younger children can gain some insight into the magnitude of the Inquest and how things have changed from carrying out a modest survey of the same kind of a modern farm or even a street.[3] Imaginative exercises, too, spring readily to mind. The compilation of the local entries by the king's officials can be dramatized and acted as a class activity, or form the basis of imaginary conversations, letters or reminiscences. The Ely Inquest provides a list of questions put by the commissioners which can be used as a basis for dramatic work.[4]

Domesday is of special value because it provides us with some basic information for many places at one particular point in time. There are other records which, while not available for so many places, can supply much more intimate details of medieval rural and manorial life. Population, social structure, agricultural and feudal administrative and judicial organization and practices can often be illustrated by local examples if not of one particular place of somewhere in the neighbourhood. One group of records—manorial custumals, rentals, and extents or surveys—provides very useful teaching material. These are often so similar in content that they may be difficult to distinguish. Frequently they list the names of tenants and give details of their land holdings, together with the rents and services (including frequency and duration) due from each, and the customs of the manor, including, for example, details of commons. Extents or surveys may also include a description of the demesne land (the part of the manor set aside for the use of the lord himself), an estimated valuation of the manor house, with its garden, vineyard, dovecote and so on, together with an estimate of the acreages of the demesne's pasture, meadow, wood and arable land. The value of any mill, fair or market may be noted and sometimes details of the cropping of the arable land, including rotation, amount of seed needed and yield. Sometimes these were domestic records of the manor or estate, sometimes they resulted from official enquiries. Many extents, for example, were attached to the inquisitions post mortem. These records are difficult to read and sometimes to translate,[5] and most teachers would be advised to seek examples among the many which have been published in local record societies' series and elsewhere. Some examples will illustrate their considerable potential for teaching purposes. The following is a translated description of the manor of Kettering (Northants.), about the year 1125:[6]

> At Kettering there are ten hides subject to royal geld. Of these 10 hides 40 villeins hold 40 virgates. These men plough in the spring four acres per virgate for the lord. Furthermore, they provide ploughs for the lord's work four times in the winter, three times in the spring and once in the summer. And these men have 22 ploughs with which they work. All these men work for the lord three days a week. Furthermore, they pay each year by custom 2s 1½d, per virgate. Together they pay 50 hens and 640 eggs. Furthermore Aelric holds 13 acres, with two acres of meadow, and pays for this 16d. And there is a mill with a miller, who pays 20s. And 8 'cotsets' who each have five acres, and they work one day a week, and make malt twice a year. And each one of them pays one penny for his goat, and if he has a she-goat a halfpenny. And there is a shepherd and a swineherd who holds eight acres. And in the ownership of the hall there are four ploughs with 32 oxen, 12 cows with 10 calves, two non-working animals, three draught horses, 300 sheep, 50 pigs, and as much additional meadow as would be worth 16s. . . .

In this description not all the peasant holders are named. Some such records, however, do this, and of course this can make them more alive to children. Thus a survey of Mileham (Norfolk) in 1301 tells us that one John Atte Fielde, a bondman, held a dwelling and thirteen acres for a rent of 2s 11d payable half at Michaelmas and half at Easter. He was obliged to attend the lord's court and to perform boon work of two ploughings in winter and spring, providing a whole plough team 'if he has one or else with part of a team'. On those days the lord provided him with twopennyworth of food. John also had to reap with one man for one day of harvest, again receiving food. A large number of his fellow villagers are named as holding their land by the same services though paying different rents for different amounts of land.[7]

1   *Cultivable land*

Southfield: $75\frac{1}{2}$ acres, $5\frac{1}{2}$ dayworks.
Opfield: 83 acres, $3\frac{3}{4}$ dayworks.
Eastfield: 165 acres, 1 rod, 3 dayworks.
'in the West' $160\frac{1}{2}$ acres, $\frac{1}{2}$ daywork.

2   *Rotation of crops*

1st field: wheat, rye, barley.
2nd field: drage, oats, beans.
3rd field: fallow.

3   *Demesne*

Area of 'curia':   7 acres, 3 rods, $6\frac{1}{2}$ dayworks.
Buildings: hall, chamber, kitchen, grange, stable, cowshed, granary.

		£	s	d
2 dovecotes	worth		10	0 p.a.
4 ovens	,,	1	6	8
2 water mills	,,	2	13	4
1 fulling mill	,,		16	0
1 fishery	,,		2	0
garden	,,		4	6
Arable land: $480\frac{1}{2}$ acres, $2\frac{1}{4}$ dayworks	,,	10	0	$2\frac{3}{4}$
Pasture land: 28 acres, 1 rod, $5\frac{1}{2}$ dayworks	,,	1	8	$4\frac{1}{2}$
Meadow (hay): $29\frac{1}{2}$ acres	,,	2	4	3
Market tolls and profits of market court	,,	1	0	0
Fines and perquisites of manorial court	,,	10	0	0
Tallage levied on tenants	,,	6	13	4
Right of way through demesne	,,		13	4
Total		37	12	$0\frac{1}{4}$

From some surveys a very detailed description of the manor can be built up. One of the manor of Wellingborough (Northants) in 1320, taken from the register of Crowland Abbey, can be summarized as on p. 98.[8]

In addition are supplied the names and status of the tenants, and details of their holdings, their money rents and other feudal obligations.

For a few counties (Bedfordshire, Buckinghamshire, Cambridgeshire, Huntingdonshire, Leicestershire, Oxfordshire, Worcestershire) the so-called hundred rolls (a hundred was a division of a county) of 1279–80 provide the same sort of information as surveys, rentals and custumals for a very large number of places. Teachers in those counties, therefore, often have available a detailed picture of a place two centuries after the Conquest which may be compared with the Domesday description. The hundred roll entries name tenants, give details of the composition of the demesne in terms of arable land, meadow, pasture and woodland, and list the sub-tenants by name with the amount of land they hold and the rents and services they owe. There is, however, the difficulty, which does not exist for Domesday, that the hundred rolls have not been published in translation. They are published in Latin in record type by the Record Commission as the *Rotuli Hundredorum*, but these volumes are likely to be found only in large libraries, and even if they are available many teachers would find translation difficult. Nevertheless where a village is known to have an entry it is likely to be so useful for teaching purposes that it is well worth going to some trouble to have a translation made. One example may serve to illustrate the wealth of detail available to the teacher who will go to the trouble of obtaining such a translation. The entry for Croxton (Cambridgeshire) describes the four estates that made up the village in 1279. The main manor, held by one Hugh, had a manor house set in eight acres with a demesne of 220 acres of arable and five of pasture. This manor had twenty-two villein tenants (all named), seventeen of them farming holdings of ten acres and five holdings of twenty acres. Eight cottager tenants (also named) held between a rood and eight acres each. All these peasants had to do boon work (and the details of this are described), but their week work had been commuted to stated money rents. Four could offer money payments in place of work at the hay harvest. In addition thirteen free tenants are named and the details of their rents and the size of their holdings are provided. For each of the three other estates similar details are given.

Because they are so lengthy such manorial records will often have to be abridged and perhaps edited a little by the teacher, and almost always he will wish to work with a translation. All this suggests that some trouble must be taken to find suitable documents in the form required. But it will usually be work well worth while, for records like these can bring to life the nature of the medieval manor and rural life in the Middle Ages far better than most textbooks. And they will provide many exercises for children of different ages and abilities. Many of the exercises suggested above for Domesday can also be applied to them, in particular the analysis and tabulation of different feudal (social) classes and their obligations. The detail provided can often form the basis of excellent dramatic and written imaginative work.[9] Moreover the study of single documents can be made to lead into the study of all sorts of general aspects of medieval history, such as farming methods, costume and feudalism. Indeed, it can form the basis for 'patch' work on medieval life locally and nationally.

Other manorial records, particularly court rolls and ministers' accounts, will fill out the picture of rural life as well as demonstrating how the manor as an institution worked. Since the manorial court administered not only petty justice but the feudal customs of the manor, its proceedings will illustrate transfer of all land held in villeinage, services, rents and other obligations of the peasantry and regulation of the open fields and other farming lands. Included, too, will be record of punishment for infringements—such as the over-stocking of the commons, the too frequent taking of wood or turf, as well as trespass with livestock on the lord's or neighbours' holdings. Other aspects of social life may also be illustrated. In the court rolls of Bradford (Yorkshire), for example, in December 1349 the effects of the Black Death are demonstrated by a long list of reliefs where new tenants took over the holdings of the deceased. One of these many entries reads as follows:

> William Couper, who held a cottage and 4 acres of bondage land there, is dead; and hereupon came Roger, his son and heir, and took those tenements to hold to him and his heirs according to the custom of the manor by the services, etc . . . and he gives to the lord 2s fine of entry.

Other entries in this court roll for the same period illustrate different aspects of manorial life and jurisdiction:[10]

> Hugh son of Thomas exercises the trade of butcher together with the trades of shoemaker and tanner. Therefore it is ordered that he be

attached to abjure those two trades, etc. Mercy, 10*d*. [An example of trades being followed without permission]

Alice Geldoghter and Adam Notebroun are bakers and sell bad bread contrary to the assize. Therefore they are in mercy. 12*d*. [An example of control of standards]

Roger son of Roger de Manynghame has made fine of ½ mark for the merchet of Cecily his wife, the lord's bondwoman; pledge, Thomas de Manynghame. [An example of merchet]

Agnes daughter of Adam atte Yate, the lord's bondwoman, has made fine for her chevage, for licence to dwell wheresoever she will, to wit, 6*d*. . . . pledge, Robert atte Yate. [An example of chevage—payment for living away from the manor]

William Notbroun and Adam Notbroun with their cattle have broken down the hedge around the lord's wood, and with the said cattle have fed off the grass of the lord's wood; therefore they are in mercy. 12*d*. [An example of trespass]

Manorial court rolls illustrate medieval village life so vividly in all its aspects that the teacher would do well to compile a set of extracts from manors in his area suitable for the age and ability of his classes. The technical and other medieval terms used in the rolls—such as heriot, mercy, virgate, curtilage, merchet, chevage—can be used in such exercises as the compilation of glossaries ('our Manorial Dictionary'), or from the basis of a series of 'cartoon' strips or wall drawings with explanations to illustrate manorial life. Court roll extracts are ideal, too, for stimulating the imagination. What we have are half-told stories, scraps of evidence, which after some study of the general background of medieval conditions can be brought to life by pupil or teacher in exercises of disciplined imagination—imaginary eye-witness accounts of the court at work, the thoughts of two disputing villagers, and so on. Even a single episode may form the basis for a class playlet, and the working of the court itself could be used for a dramatic exercise to good effect.[11] Again, a set of character studies can be compiled, with perhaps drawings illustrating costume and housing. For social studies comparison with later and with modern courts and local government institutions may follow.

Taken with secondary works these records and others, such as lay subsidies and poll tax returns, and the study of physical remains such as churches, castles and monasteries (Chapter 8), can provide a wealth of local material to illustrate the normal teaching of medieval rural history.

Medieval and early modern town life

Town life is a commonly taught topic, and the possibility of using local examples for the medieval and early modern period depends to some extent on the existence in the area of an ancient borough. The aspects of town history in these periods for which local illustration may profitably be sought include the growth and nature of local government, the gild system, markets and fairs, housing and living conditions, topography and demography. Usually a teacher will have at hand published histories of local towns, so that he will have more to guide him and to build on than when he treats rural villages. These works will often indicate the existence of original records, and older histories often print extracts from them. Published editions of town records are quite likely to exist, too.

The earliest reference to a town may well be in Domesday. This source and the materials available for the study of physical growth, population, housing and living conditions are described elsewhere. The development of self-government in towns goes hand-in-hand with emancipation from feudal control. For most boroughs local historians will already have traced the growth of liberties and independence, and the substance of the local story will be known. The records concerned with such changes will provide good illustrative material. The achievement of liberties was legally recognized in 'charters' of privileges. The whereabouts of printed editions of the borough charters should be known to local libraries, and indeed many towns have had their charters published in full or abbreviated form. Otherwise the three volumes of *British Borough Charters* may be consulted. These summarize the content of charters with comments, indicating where copies can be found in print.[12]

The more intimate details of the workings of town government and of town life generally may best be illustrated from the minute books of borough councils. These exist more commonly for the early modern period than for medieval times, and are often not too difficult to read in the original. For some boroughs, however, published editions exist.[13] The content of council minute books varies, but generally they record the election of officers and the appointment of officials, all the meetings of the council, those present and the decisions taken. Sometimes, but not always, they will indicate the thinking behind the decisions. Since the councils were concerned with almost every aspect of town life, their minutes are full of useful material for class use. So miscellaneous are the entries, however, that the teacher would be well advised to compile his own sets of extracts rather than to get children to work directly from originals or full copies. There will usually be plenty of good examples to bring to life the generalizations of the textbook on town life. The harshness of punishments for petty misdemeanours, for example, is colourfully illustrated by the following extract from the Liverpool town book for 1565, concerning a pickpocket:[14]

This yere Sundaye at nyght after soper, the ixth of this Decembre, was oon Patrick Fyn, an Ireshe borne in the Queyne's Countrie [Queen's County], lakye, late in therle of Ormonde's liverie, owt of service taken in mayster [   ]s howse for cuttyng a purse of oone of the fyne gentilmen that went to Ireland wyth my lord deputie Sidney's campayne, in which was jowels and gold to the value of v *li.*, all had agayne, for he was takyn with the purse in the same howse before mentioned. And he was prisoned that nyght, and after his examinacion neylid to a post by the eare and soe whipped owt of towne nagyed from the myddyll upwardes.

The following illustration of town life and its regulation by the borough council are taken from the Exeter council's minute books, but are typical of what is to be found in the records of other boroughs:

9 March 1555	That Exbridge shalbe pavyd this yer and one of the peers plankyd.
21 March 1556	That the sale of Rawe cloath hereafter shalbe kypte in the Northgate Street from Watbury Street downewards towards Northgate and nott elswere.
12 December 1558	That the markett for the pultry, eggs, piggs, butter, chese, capons, ducks, hennys and other victuall of olde tyme accustomyd, to be sold at the Greyt Conduit and uppwarde accordyng as it hath byn usyd.
15 February 1537	That there schalle no Bruer send owte any ale of there howses withyn xxiiij oures after that hit ys tunnyd upon payment of every Borell 12*d.*

A great variety of other records are likely to exist for many boroughs. There may, for example, be memoranda or 'remembrance' books, known as custumals, like the Little and Great Red Books of Bristol, in which important laws and ordinances and other significant matters affecting the town are recorded. Freemen's books or rolls, apprenticeship records, poor-law records, and the records of the various borough courts—mayor's court, orphans' court, manor or leet court, quarter sessions—may also be available, sometimes reproduced in print by record societies (see also below).

Markets and fairs were an aspect of early town life that history teachers rightly emphasize. Most histories of older towns will probably give some information on these, but some useful teaching material can be found elsewhere. The markets and fairs recorded in Domesday in a county or region can be listed and mapped,[15] as well as those included in local borough charters. A parliamentary paper, the first report of the Royal Commission on Market Rights and Tolls (1888), records the details of all royal grants of markets and fairs made between 1199 and 1483, and this will be worth searching out. Details of such matters as the dates and duration of fairs are indicated in charters and changes in these in further grants. Occasionally fuller information on fairs and markets is available in miscellaneous printed sources. We have, for example, the form of the proclamations opening fairs at Manchester, Sheffield, York, Stourbridge, Southampton and other towns. Sometimes the proceedings of fair courts have been published. These can provide down-to-earth human stories, where little incidents are caught for all time, as in the court records of St Ives (Huntingdonshire) fair in 1312:[16]

> Whereas it has been found that John of Reading sold to Robert of Bedford two bales of licorice and warranted it to him as good and pure, and afterwards the said Robert found that this licorice was not so good and pure as the sample which the said John first showed to the said Robert in making the sale, and not uniform therewith; therefore inquest is to be made by the merchants whether the said licorice ought to be forfeited to the use of the lord king or not according to merchant law and custom, etc.

For the early modern period council minute books will often contain information on markets and fairs, and sometimes the writings of travellers contain comments. An extract from Thomas Baskerville's lengthy and vivid description of the hustle and bustle of the market at Norwich in 1681 is worth quoting.[17]

> These people fill a square of ground on the side of a hill twice as big Abingdon market place . . . only allowing room for single persons to pass between; and above these the butchers have their shambles and such kind of people as sell fish, of which there was plenty of such kinds as the seas hereabouts afford, viz. crabs, flounders, mackerel, very cheap, but lobster for sea fish and pike or jack for river fish were dear enough. They asked me for one pike under 2 foot, 2s. 6d., and for a pot of pickled oysters they would have a shilling. Here I saw excellent oatmeal which

being curiously hulled looked like French barley, with great store of gingerbread and other edible things.

One aspect of early town life usually stressed in school is the gilds and their activities. The right to possess a gild may be found in borough charters, but often it is not easy to obtain much information about individual gilds until the early modern period. Existing town histories may well have something to say about them, and these should, of course, be consulted. In addition, J. Toulmin Smith's *English Gilds* (1870) prints a large number of replies made by gilds in the late fourteenth century to a royal enquiry into their rules, practices and property. An extract from new regulations sought by the fullers' gild of Bristol will serve to show just how useful this book is:

> First, it is ordained that, each year, four men of the craft shall be chosen as Masters, to search every house of the said craft, twice a-week, and oversee all defects in the said cloths, . . . and to present them before you at the court; so that whosoever does such bad work shall pay for the same the full price of the cloth; one half to go to the town, and the other half to the craft, . . . and this, over and above all reasonable amends made to the buyer of the cloths. Also, the Masters of the craft shall not give more to the men of the said craft than fourpence a-day, [in summer] and threepence a-day [in winter], And if any of the masters pays more . . . he shall be fined, each time, ij.*s.*; . . . And if the men take more from the masters, they shall pay, each time, xij.*d.*; . . . And if the men are rebels or contrarious, and will not work, then the four masters shall have power to take them before the Mayor . . .

Municipal records, too, may include useful material on craft gilds, for such gilds grew up under the control of borough councils. Ordinances are usually recorded and much miscellaneous matter. The Norwich mayor's court has, for example, the following entry in 1524:[18]

> John Howse, Taillour, is accused by the wardens of the taillours craft for that he would not suffre the said wardens to serch in his shoppe in causes concernyng the occupation of taillours craft, and also for defaute of workemanship of a kirtill and a peticote founden by the warden of [the] occupacion and other mysdemenours. Whereupon he is ffined xvi*d* and to giff to the occupacion a pound candell of wax.

Other examples can be obtained from the domestic records of gilds, which are often now to be found in print. Ordinances, minutes of meetings and financial accounts will provide good material to illustrate the organization, the policy and the social, philanthropic and economic functions of the gilds.

Thus the teacher seeking to illustrate lessons on medieval and early modern town life is likely, if he will spend some time, to be able to collect good examples for many of the aspects he wishes to stress. Records such as those mentioned above can be used not only for pure illustration or 'lead in' materials but in some cases as a basis for work cards and other exercises. Town life as a topic lends itself to the project approach at various age levels. If sufficient local examples can be found, and if general reference works too can be provided, the compilation by groups or individuals of a complete booklet dealing with different aspects of town life can be undertaken. This can be augmented by large illustrative drawings and plans for display on walls or in folders—as, for example, types of houses and shops, inns, gates, public buildings like almshouses, gildhalls and market buildings, and parish churches. Churches usually survive and in some places other buildings too, and these may be visited. Where they do not they may have been recorded in pictures or photographs.

The need for fieldwork (see Chapter 8) in such exercises is obvious. Remaining buildings can be sketched, photographed and plotted on maps; copies of older drawings and photographs of both extant and disappeared buildings can be sought in local libraries. Map work, too, can be undertaken, using old street plans. Comparisons with the present-day street pattern can be made. Pupils may also construct maps of the whole area, indicating the significant towns of the period: which had markets and fairs, which had gilds, which had charters, and so on.

The titles of the main officials and officers of the town can be discovered from the council minutes; their actual names can be noted, too, and their duties investigated. This may form the basis of a comparison with the structure of modern local government. By early modern times it may be possible to begin the compilation of biographies of local worthies for a 'Dictionary of Local Biography' which can be continued and added to as the class passes to the study of later periods. Likewise a period time chart setting important local events against national ones can be started. Traditional essay work on town life with local examples can, of course, be undertaken by pupils of various ages, but I have quoted sufficient examples above to indicate that local records will often provide stimulating material for different kinds of imaginative work: playlets of the town council in session, of the gild searchers at work, of the trial and punishment of misdemeanours in various courts, of the life of markets and fairs. Written eye-witness accounts, 'newspaper' reports, diaries and the like can all be stimulated by such local documentary examples as I have quoted. Where, as in junior and middle schools, sufficient time for ambitious practical work is available, the construction of large-scale models and maps with accompanying booklet guides or classroom friezes illustrating aspects of town life are worthwhile and rewarding.[19]

Farming and rural life from Tudor times

Aspects of rural life generally emphasized in the school history syllabus include the Tudor and Stuart enclosure movement, especially where it led to depopulation and the expansion of sheep farming, the later parliamentary enclosure movement, the effects of the French wars on agriculture, improvements in farming methods and organization in the modern period, and the standard of life of different classes in the rural community. For many such topics of national history the teacher should be able to find interesting local material for illustration. Some of those discussed in Chapter 5 may also be relevant here, while others are now suggested.

Records of returns to the commission investigating early Tudor enclosures are available in print in I. S. Leadam's *Domesday of Inclosures* (1897), available in large libraries. The following report on Little Wigborough (Essex) illustrates the value of this book:

> Item whe fynd that ther ys a farme of Sir Roberd Cotton Knygh late deseesed within the parrech aforsaid caled Copedhall and Maner plase therof ys decaid and pulled doun by the said Sir Robert and non Inabytacyon wher Ther was wont to be kept on yt a good howseeld and ferm lond plowid and now lyeys no lond plowyd nor in howsold vse wher ther was wont to be kept in yt a fermer and his wyfe and xviij or xx personys fownde on yt and now yt is reterned to pasteur and graseng and the tenaunt and his wyfe kepyth and the fermer thereof ys won Wylliam hyll of Soffolk Marchant and yt hath leye to paster thys xvij yers.

Probate inventories for rural areas for the sixteenth and seventeenth centuries are excellent for classroom use. They show what yeomen's and other farmers' dwellings were like, and the types of material possessions they had. In addition farm tools, livestock, dung, grain in store and sometimes acreages of growing crops are listed, and these give an idea of farming activities. Hearth and poll tax records for the seventeenth century can be used to show the stratification of wealth in rural parishes.[20] And for some places there may be farmers' diaries or accounts to add to the detail. Some of these have been printed, like the notebooks of Henry Best of the East Riding, from which the following is an extract:[21]

> Wee usually sell our wool att hoame, unlesse it bee by chance that wee carry some to Beverley on Midsummer day: those that buy it carry it into the West, towards Leeds, Hallifax, and Wakefield. They bringe [with them] packe-horses, and carry it away in greate packes; these wool-men come and goe continually from clipping time till Michaele-masse. Those that have pasture wooll sell usually for 10s. and 11s. a stone; and oftentimes, when woll is very deare, for 12s. a stone; but our faugh sheepe do not afforde so find a wooll, whearefore wee seldome sell for above 8s. or 9s. a stone, unlesse it bee by chance when wooll is very deare that wee reach to 10s. a stone, or very neare. Woolmen dislike and finde greate falt with woll that hath much salve or tarre in it, and likewise with that which is eyther blacke for want of goode washinge. . . .

For the sixteenth to the eighteenth centuries a common type of source of potential value for teaching purposes is the record of the assessment of farm workers' wages by the Justices of the Peace. Many wage assessments have been published by record societies, and originals, found in quarter-sessions records in local record offices, are not difficult to read or transcribe. The following Warwickshire assessment was made in 1738:[22]

> The particular rate of wages of all manner of artificers, labourers, and servants, as well by the day with meat and drink as without, as also by the whole year in gross or by task, made and provided, having a special regard and consideration to the prices of provisions and all other circumstances necessary to be considered at this time. April, 1738.

	£	s	d
Every head servant in husbandry by the year	5	10	0
Second servant ,, ,, ,,	4	0	0
Servant boy from 14 to 18 years of age ,,	2	10	0
Servant boy from 11 to 14 ,, ,, ,,	1	0	0
Every head servant maid by the year	3	0	0
Second maid servant ,, ,,	2	10	0
Labourers from Martinmas to March 25 by the day	0	0	8
From March 25 to harvest and after harvest to Martinmas	0	0	9
Every mower of grass by the day, with drink	0	1	0
,, ,, without drink ,,	0	1	2
Every woman in haymaking, with drink	0	0	5
,, ,, without drink	0	0	6

Every woman in corn harvest, with drink	o	o	6
„ „ without drink	o	o	7
Every carpenter by the day March 25 to St. Michael's, with drink	o	1	o
„ „ without drink	o	1	2
From Michaelmas to Lady Day, with drink	o	o	10
„ „ without drink	o	1	o
Every mason by the day in summer, with drink	o	o	10
„ „ without drink	o	1	o
Every mason by the day in winter, with drink	o	o	10
„ „ without drink	o	1	o
Thatcher by day, summer and winter	o	1	o
Weeders of corn by the day	o	o	4

Whether local material to illustrate parliamentary enclosure of the eighteenth and early nineteenth centuries is available near the town or village in which a particular school is situated will depend on the locality. Local record offices in many counties and towns will, however, be able to produce enclosure maps and awards for somewhere in the vicinity which will record the redistributed allotments and sometimes the old open fields or commons, as has been described more fully in Chapter 4. Enclosure records are invaluable for class use, and though pupils should if possible be given a chance to see original documents and maps it will probably be more convenient for work to be done from photocopies. Using these in conjunction with modern OS maps, much work on the topographical aspects of the area can be undertaken. Used with literary evidence of farming in the area they can provide considerable insight into the enclosure movement generally and its effect on agricultural change. A Hampshire secondary school was able to find records of two contrasting local enclosures, the one demonstrating 'land-grabbing at its worst' and the other relating to a place where reasonable provision for copy- and leaseholders had been made. The documents, photographed and made into slides, illustrated the pre-enclosure and post-enclosure structure and led pupils and their parents to seek out and study other local enclosure awards.[23]

The teacher will need to make a careful study of available enclosure records before deciding which to use, and he should make quite sure he himself comprehends the documents before attempting to use them with a class. Usually it will be necessary for him to introduce a study of the maps, awards and schedules to the children rather carefully to make sure they are understood before proceeding further. If the area is today still rural, and sometimes if it is not, it should, if possible, be visited by the class, and studied, too, from a modern OS map to get an idea of subsequent changes. The discerning eye will often find boundaries established by the enclosure that are still followed, or evidence of ridge-and-furrow or older boundaries fossilized perhaps in the direction of modern streets or lanes. The opportunity for a variety of map work (see also Chapter 4) and descriptive writing is obvious. Models and maps can be made to record the pre- and post-enclosure pattern, large-scale coloured overhead projector transparencies can be made, perhaps to superimpose the new on the old, and so on. Tables of landholders before and after enclosure can be compiled, and information from directories used as supplementary evidence. There is scope, too, for imaginative work, stimulated by the records, on the likely social impact of enclosure on village life. The visit of the commissioners, for example, can form the basis of both written imaginative work and dramatic activity. It may be salutary, if enclosure took place in the nineteenth century, to look at the population figures from the published censuses to see whether in fact the traditional textbook picture of rural depopulation subsequent to enclosure is to be found.

It is not difficult to find local examples to illustrate the improved agriculture traditionally associated with the enclosure movement. The writings of Arthur Young and William Marshall, and the *General Views of Agriculture* (Chapter 5) are full of useful and vivid material.

The agricultural distress of the post-1815 period can be illustrated in some areas from a Board of Agriculture publication, *The Agricultural State of the Kingdom in . . . 1816*, recently reprinted (ed. G. Mingay, 1970), and from records relating to poor relief (Chapter 7). The fortunes of agriculture then and in the later nineteenth century may also be illustrated from a variety of parliamentary papers (see Chapter 5) and the published censuses. These will show a decline in population in many rural and market towns. Thus in Devon between 1861 and 1891 the population of 208 rural parishes fell by anything up to 60 per cent.

The details of life on the farm in the nineteenth century can be illustrated by local exercises without difficulty. Those parliamentary papers containing reports of the employment of women and children in agriculture have many vivid first-hand records of life from the point of view of employer and employed. In many parts of the country museums of rural life have been set up, and visits to these can be brought into the study of farm machinery and implements. Farm accounts, advertisements, sale catalogues and the like exist in many record offices, and it is worth while examining them for possible teaching material for both the nineteenth and the twentieth centuries.

For notes to this chapter see pp. 169–70.

7 Local history to illustrate national history: II

The relief of poverty

The history of poor relief forms a part of many history syllabuses and is also often treated as background for investigation of the Welfare State in social studies courses. Though there were many local variations within the framework of the national poor law, it is doubtful whether regional differences should often be stressed at school level. Of course, the teacher will need to point to such major variations as existed between northern industrial areas and the rural south following the Poor Law Amendment Act of 1834, and to special Acts setting up individual arrangements in major towns, as happened at Bristol in the seventeenth century. Usually, however, it will be possible to illustrate the general national story without distorting local history. And for most parts of the country there is a wealth of good teaching material. For official relief of poverty before 1834 the main sources are parish or town records. It may be that the duties of the overseers of the poor—the local executive officers—can be illustrated from an actual confirmation of their appointment, like the following:[1]

> We whose names are hereunto subscribed, Justices of the Peace for the County of Stafford . . . do approve and appoint Thomas Higgs, William Burleigh, William Dawes and Thomas Ash being Substantial House holders in the parish of Gnosall to be Overseers of the Poor . . . for one whole Year next ensuing the Date hereof, Commanding you together with the Church-Wardens, to provide for the said Poor, by meeting together, once every Month, to take Order for their Relief, and to set all the Poor to Work that are able, by providing a convenient Stock of some Ware of Stuff in your Parish for that Purpose: And you place out as Apprentices all such Children as are fit to place out and whose Parents are unable to maintain them; and that you provide necessary Relief for all such Poor as are Lame, Old, Blind, and Impotent, and unable to work; but that you relieve no Persons whatsoever, not wearing your Parish Badge. Hereof fail not at your Perils. Given under our Hands and Seales this 27th Day of May in the Year of Our Lord, One Thousand, Seven Hundred and Sixty.

The financial accounts of the overseers, often available in print or manuscript, can be used to demonstrate how relief was given, the sort of people who received it, and the sources of revenue; for the poor rate was not the only source—some parishes accumulated a 'poor stock' from gifts, and sometimes paternity fines were channelled into poor relief.[2] In the following extract from the Ipswich overseers' accounts[3] children might be expected to deduce the policy of outdoor relief, to notice that many of the recipients were widows, probably elderly, that the town paid for the boarding out of destitute (probably orphaned) children, that there was a 'sick house', that there was not a flat rate of relief, and so on. Other such records often show expenditure on clothing, medical attention, nursing, burials, schooling and even laundry. By using a document like this the nature of the system is more likely to be understood than from the generalizations of a textbook.

Payde to the poore within the towne the xxth daye of December 1577 for the weke paste:

St Margarete's	Wedow Byet	2*d*.
	Thomas Harpam	4*d*.
	Wedow Collen	6*d*.
	Wedow Cocsedge	2*d*.
	Wedow Butler	1*d*.
	Wylliam Daye	4*d*.
	Edmund Haule	4*d*.
	Wylliam Thornell	2*d*.
	Wedow Thunder	4*d*.
	John Lee, at nurce with Carpynder	12*d*.
St Clemente's	Father Holmes and hys wyfe	12*d*.
	John Brunnyng, for kepyng a chylde	12*d*.
St Peter's	Peter Rowland	10*d*.
	Wedow Cutberd	10*d*.
	Rose Dutnalle	8*d*.
	Nykolas Pynchebacke, for kepyng a chylde	8*d*.
	Wedow Edwardes, at the Syckhowse	7*d*.
	Elyzabeth Wyllet, at the Syckhowse	7*d*.
	Wedow Balles, at the Syckhowse	10*d*.

Separate accounts were kept of the levying and collection of the poor rate, and these can be used to show the incidence of this tax. Local examples of such experiments as the 'labour rate', the 'roundsman system', and the 'Speenhamland system' can sometimes be found in vestry minute books[4] or in general descriptions, such as Eden's *State of the Poor*[5] (a book full of good teaching material), the *General Views of Agriculture* (Chapter 5), and the Poor Law Commissioners' report of 1834 (a parliamentary paper). Eden also has very detailed information on workhouses in different places, and the following is an example for St Martin in the Fields, London:

> The poor of this parish are partly relieved at home, and partly maintained in the workhouse in Castle-street, Leicester Fields. There are, at present, about 240 weekly out-pensioners, besides a considerable number of poor on the casual list. Of 573, the number of poor at present in the workhouse, 473 are adults and 100 children; of which 54 are boys, 21 girls, able to work, and 25 infants. Their principal employment is spinning flax, picking hair, carding wool, etc.; their annual earnings, on an average of a few years past, amount to about £150. It was once attempted to establish a manufacture in the house; but the badness of the situation for business, the want of room for workshops, and the difficulty of compelling the able poor to pay proper attention to work, rendered the project unsuccessful. Between 70 and 80 children belonging to this parish are, generally, out at nurse in the country: a weekly allowance of 3s. (lately advanced to 3s. 6d.) is paid with each child. At 7 or 8 years of age, the children are taken into the house, and taught a little reading, etc., for three or four years, and then put out apprentices.

Sometimes, especially in urban areas, workhouse accounts may exist for this period, and if so they too can be used to illustrate such interesting matters as the regulation, diet and accommodation of the inmates. Details of the establishments of a more penal nature—the houses of correction or bridewells—in the late eighteenth and early nineteenth centuries may be found in John Howard's *State of the Prisons* (various editions). These are often suitable for school use.

Schoolchildren often find the workings of the settlement system hard to comprehend, and the use of actual documentary evidence serves to show how it worked. It should not be difficult to find local examples. Constables'[6] and overseers' accounts will give details, and often actual settlement certificates and passes survive. Settlement certificates enabled persons to move about by providing a written guarantee that their native parish would receive them back if they became paupers. Passes indicated that vagrants had been punished and should be allowed free passage to their parish of origin. Since the magistrates had supervision of the poor law, quarter-sessions records, which exist in large numbers, are full of illustrations of the poor law at work. It was the JPs, for example, who decided which parish was responsible for a particular pauper and issued orders for dealing with cases. The West Riding sessions rolls for 1598 contain such items as:[7]

Whereas this Court is informed that a poore Woman & a Yonge Child came begging into the Towneshipp of Northowrom about a moneth since, & staied ther forwer or five daies untill the said woman did fall extreamely sicke & then the Constable of the said Towne did carry the said woman, being at poynt of death, & her child unto a poore mans house within the Towneshipp of Shelf, wher the said woman within three howers after died, by meanes wherof the said Child being not past a yeare old is still in the said towne of Shelf, which is far unable to releive the same by reason they are alreadie overcharged with their owne poore: Yt is therfore ordered that the Inhabitantes within the Towne-shipp of Northowrom shall pay xij*d* and Shelfe iiij*d* weekelie towards the releif and educacion of the said Child and it to remayne within the Towne of Shelfe untill further order be taken herein.

Particularly useful for teaching purposes are the records of examin-ations of paupers by the Justices, which are to be found in quarter-sessions records. These sorry documents can bring understanding to today's pupils of the nature of working-class life in this period as few other types of records can, for they provide autobiographies of a class of people for whom such details are not normally available. The following is an example from a Staffordshire parish:[8]

The Examination of Francis Evans of the parish of Gnosall . . . labourer . . . 11th day of June, 1774 . . . This Examinant saith, That he was born in the parish of Gnosall . . . which was the place of his fathers settlement. That Twenty years since or thereabouts he was hired to Mr. Butler of the parish of Claybrook in the county of Leicester for Eleven months which he served. That his master then hired him again for eight pounds a year and they then agreed that this examinant should be absent from the service a week in some part of the year—to prevent his gaining a settlement when his master could best spare him—That he continued with Mr. Butler upon his farm in Claybrook . . . for two years except a week in each year which time he came to see his friends in Staffordshire and his master hired a Labourer in his room to do his work, and stopped such Labourers pay out of this examinants wages in each of the two last mentioned years. That since the said service in the parish of Claybrook he hath not to his knowledge & belief done any act whereby he could gain a settlement And that he hath a wife named Mary and three children namely Francis aged about seven years, Elizabeth aged about four years and Joseph about one year & three months old now residing in the parish of Gnosall aforesaid ———

Sworn the day & year first
before written before us——

	The mark of
John Williamson	**X**
John Turton	Francis Evans

The basis of relief was changed by the Poor Law Amendment Act of 1834, Unions taking the place of single parishes as the local units of administration, and elected guardians replacing parish officers as administrators. For the nineteenth century there are many published parliamentary papers dealing with poor relief before and after 1834, and these are a source for many good examples for teaching purposes.[9] The state of affairs on the eve of the 1834 Act is, for example, described in the report of the Royal Commission on the Poor Law containing detailed descriptions of places all over the country. A little later we have the reports of a select committee set up to investigate how the Act was working. Then there are the annual reports (1835–1919) of the central body set up to supervise the local boards of guardians—successively the Poor Law Commission, the Poor Law Board and the Local Government Board. All sorts of detailed information, fascinating and illuminating for classroom use, can be found in these volumes. The following is an extract for Bury St Edmunds Union in 1871 (*P.L. Bd. 23rd Rep.*):

> This Union contains two parishes, covering 2,934 acres with a population in 1861 of 13,318, and its total pauperism on the 14th April 1870 was 888, or 6.7 per cent on its population. This pauperism consisted of 371 old and infirm, 181 able-bodied, and 336 children. The workhouse contained (it is a very old and defective house) at the date named 99 inhabitants of whom 41 per old and infirm, 20 were able-bodied, and 38 were children; 23 boys attended the workhouse school, of whom 10 received industrial training.
>
> Out-relief is administered at the rate of 83 per cent in money, and 17 per cent in kind. The average weekly relief given to an out-door pauper is 1s. $6\frac{6}{10}d.$, and the average weekly cost of an in-door pauper is 3s. $0\frac{4}{10}d.$ . . . .

Minute books of the local union boards of guardians may exist in the local record office, and though unlikely to have been published they will certainly be worth looking at for further details of life in the workhouse, and will usually be quite legible for pupils.[10]

Clearly if the poor law studied through the ordinary school text-

DIETARY for Able-bodied MEN and WOMEN in the *Woburn* Workhouse, from the 21st January 1837 to the present time.

		BREAKFAST.		DINNER.				SUPPER.		
		Bread.	Gruel.	Cooked Meat.	Cooked Potatoes in their skins.	Soup.	Suet or Rice Pudding.	Bread.	Cheese or Butter.	Broth.
		oz.	*pints.*	*oz.*	*lbs.*	*pints.*	*oz.*	*oz.*	*oz.*	*pints.*
Sunday	Men	6	1½	4	1	–	–	6	1	–
	Women	5	1½	4	1	–	–	5	1	–
Monday	Men	6	1½	–	½	1½	–	6	1	–
	Women	5	1½	–	½	1½	–	5	1	–
Tuesday	Men	6	1½	4	1	–	–	6	1	–
	Women	5	1½	4	1	–	–	5	1	–
Wednesday	Men	6	1½	–	½	1½	–	6	1	–
	Women	5	1½	–	½	1½	–	5	1	–
Thursday	Men	6	1½	4	1	–	–	6	–	1½
	Women	5	1½	4	1	–	–	5	–	1½
Friday	Men	6	1½	–	–	–	16	6	1	–
	Women	5	1½	–	–	–	14	5	1	–
Saturday	Men	6	1½	–	½	1½	–	6	1	–
	Women	5	1½	–	½	1½	–	5	1	–

Old people of 60 years of age and upwards may be allowed on meat-days, 2 oz. of bread in lieu of half the quantity of potatoes; and on soup-days, 4 oz. of bread, instead of potatoes, for dinner; as also the able-bodied women, when actually employed in washing.

Old people, as above, may be allowed tea in the following quantities: 1 oz. each per week to a number not exceeding seven; 7 oz. to a number exceeding seven, and not exceeding nine; 8 oz. to a number exceeding nine, and not exceeding 11; 7 oz. of butter and 8 oz. of sugar each per week, instead of gruel for breakfast.

Able-bodied women employed in washing may be allowed at the rate of half an oz. of tea and 3 oz. of sugar each, for every three days actually so employed, in lieu of gruel for breakfast, if so desired.

Children under nine years of age to be dieted at discretion; above nine, to be allowed the same quantities as women.

Sick, to be dieted as directed by the medical officer.

January 31, 1838.

(signed) *William Cole*, Clerk.

3 Extract from the twentieth report of the Select Committee on the Poor Law Amendment Act (British Parliamentary Paper, 1837–8)

book is a dull, often incomprehensible affair, largely concerned with dates and Acts, there is a great deal of scope for providing real insight through the use of interesting local source material, even if used solely as illustration. But, of course, such documents will have more varied uses. They can be used as comprehension exercises with attached work cards or in social studies to compare with aspects of modern welfare services. Above all, these very human documents are so evocative, and at a level likely to touch children's sympathy, that they provide excellent material on which to base stories, newspaper reports, diaries, playlets and other imaginative work. For older children an excellent exercise for historical training is to get children to write parallel accounts of the same incidents from the point of view of the pauper and his family and from that of the magistrates, officials and payers of the poor rate. In both junior and secondary classes following history or social studies courses single documents can also provoke considerable discussion on the nature of poverty and the responsibility of the community, and on such matters as changing social attitudes.

Older secondary pupils, using material taken from such records as parliamentary papers and poor-law overseers' accounts, can compile tables of statistics and graphs of poverty and the expenditure involved to see how they relate to periods of economic distress or national legislation.[11] In some places there may be scope for visits, especially if the old workhouse is still standing, as is often the case. There may also be local almshouses, which, with visits to the parish church—where there may be painted wall boards giving information on local charities—would open up a field of investigation I have not here touched on: the extent and nature of private charity.[12] Local photographic collections may provide examples for the later nineteenth and early twentieth centuries of the interiors of workhouses and their inmates. Indeed, study of local poor relief records of one kind or another can provide a way of introducing children to a detailed investigation, as a 'line of development', or as a chronological 'patch', of the life of those at the lower levels of society.

Aspects of modern political and religious history

Many secondary schools follow history syllabuses largely concerned with national political history, for which local history and source materials are readily available. The aspects covered and the sort of sources available are, however, so numerous and disparate that only general advice can be given here. Moreover the time available for local history in such circumstances is frequently limited, so that often its use is confined largely to the provision of purely illustrative examples, or as a lead-in to the general history being studied. Often, however, the material can be used also for deductive, descriptive and imaginative work of the same kind as described elsewhere.

Certain parts of the country had particular significance in events of national importance—the christianization of Britain, the murder of Becket, the castles of Edward I, Kett's rebellion, the Armada, Monmouth's rebellion, the Jacobite risings, the troubles of 1816–19, Chartism, Dunkirk and the 'blitz', to name only a few. The teacher may find enough in good local histories to provide the local illustrations he needs for his national themes. For recent times the famous Plymouth 'bomb' street map, with each dot marking the site of at least one high-explosive bomb dropped on the city in the Second World War,[13] can bring to the consciousness of children what their older fellow citizens experienced in the war. The devastating raid on Coventry on 14–15 November 1940 connected local history with international, for it was partly a retaliation for the British attack on Berlin during the Hitler–Molotov talks.[14] For those towns which, like Plymouth and Coventry, suffered such attacks, published accounts as well as contemporary newspaper reports usually exist.

From Tudor times at least, however, the teacher can, with a little trouble, illustrate aspects of national history from colourful local source material even when the locality concerned had no special connection with the events. For the early period the teacher can often find local material in the published volumes of the *Letters and Papers of Henry VIII*, the *Calendar of State Papers, Domestic* and the *Acts of the Privy Council*. The reports of the Historical Manuscripts Commission on local record collections also often print in full or calendar form similarly useful records. For the eighteenth and nineteenth centuries local newspapers and parliamentary papers are an almost boundless source of good printed teaching material, not too difficult to obtain. For this period there are usually also local collections of political posters and the like.

From the sixteenth century onwards, too, such types of source as town-council minute books, quarter-sessions records and episcopal visitations, all of which sometimes appear in print, may provide useful teaching material. I cannot here deal with every aspect of national political history for which local illustration is possible. A few examples however, may be given.

Many of the political events of the sixteenth and seventeenth centuries were concerned with religious matters. For some areas it is possible to find good material for the dissolution of the monasteries and friaries. Some local record societies have published surveys and other records which can throw light on the activities of the monasteries before the dissolution, and some have published actual suppression papers from the originals in the Public Record Office. The PRO *Letters and Papers of Henry VIII* also print many of these. They provide excellent teaching material. The following plea from the Abbot of York to Thomas Cromwell in 1539 is an example:[15]

> Right honorable . . . lord, in my most humble maner I recommend me to your good lordshipe, evenso thankyng the same for your synguler goodnes towardes me and this poore house at all tymes, besechyng the same of contynuance in this my greate necessitie, and if it myght please the Kynges most graciouse maiestye that this his monasterye myght stande with alterations to serue his hignes . . . than I humblye becyche you to be so good lord to me as to assigne me a good pensione and a honest house to dwell yn in this my age and weyknesse of bodye, yf it may be the maner of Overton, with thapportenances; to be had to me as parcell of my pensione as the valor therof shall extende, and as I am boundon I shall contynually pray for your good lordshipe long to contynow in myche honor. At York the ixth day of November.

> Yowr lorshippes humble Beadsman, William Abbott ther.

Often, of course, the ruins of monastic houses still remain and some of their buildings are now, as at Chester, cathedrals and churches. Clearly there is considerable scope here for a combination of literary work in the classroom and fieldwork (Chapter 8).

Many local historical and record societies have published documents for the sixteenth and seventeenth centuries concerning recusancy, Puritanism and dissent generally. G. Lyon Turner's *Original Records of Early Nonconformity* (1911) contains examples of the existence of dissenting conventicles in 1665 and 1669 in many parts of the country: at North Curry (Somerset) there were in 1669 three conventicles, a Puritan preacher and combined dissenting congregations of 340 persons. Numbers of adult Anglicans, Roman Catholics and Puritans in 1676, parish by parish, can be obtained for many places from the Compton census (Chapter 5). Other Anglican records, sometimes now in print, provide more detailed and lively information, as, for example, the accusation that the vicar of Childerditch (Essex) in 1605 would not wear the surplice, 'doth not use the sign of the Cross in baptism', and refused to read the Prayer Book.[16] The volumes of the *Calendar of State Papers, Domestic* covering this period can provide even more colourful material for teaching the politico-religious history of the early modern period. The following description of the discovery in 1665 of a conventicle at Orchard Portman (Somerset) is such an example:

> Two Deputy Lieutenants of Somersetshire to Lord Arlington. Having notice of a great conventicle, got some servants, broke open the doors, and took 60 men and as many women; sent the men to the Sessions, where they were convicted and some paid, others went to gaol. Among them are 11 ministers living in or near Taunton, and there are as many more who preach up and down, and are so close in their meetings that they cannot be heard of till over; the head layman is Mr Malleck, a man of fortune, who keeps a nonconforming minister in his house.

The English Civil War and its antecedents form a part of many school history syllabuses, and much of the country was affected by the military and political events connected with that upheaval. Aspects of the personal rule of Charles I can often be illustrated at a local level from the volumes of the *Acts of the Privy Council* and those of the *Calendar of State Papers, Domestic*, together with other such published works as the *Calendar of Clarendon State Papers in the Bodleian Library* (5 vols., Oxford, 1872–1970). These and such publications as Clarendon's *History of the Great Rebellion* (various editions), and the *Writings and Speeches of Oliver Cromwell* (various editions) have much on the war itself, too, and the events of the Interregnum. There is indeed a great deal of contemporary local material concerning the war available in print which is useful in teaching. We have to hand, for example, many accounts of battles. Some of these are straightforward descriptions of events. Colonel Slingsby's recollections of the battle of Landsdown and Roundway Down is one of these. The following, taken from its first page, is sufficient to indicate how useful a basis such works may provide for secondary-school children for map work, imaginative writing, diagrams, and as a lead into further work in the library.[17]

> The night before the battaile att Launsdowne the Kings Army quarter'd att Marsfield; in the morning betimes Waller sent a strong party of horse towardes our head quarter, who beate in all our horse guards, and alarum'd all our quarters: wee instantly drew into the field and march two miles towardes Launsdowne where we could see the Rebells Army drawne up upon the top of the hill, he stood upon a piece of ground almost inaccessible. In the brow of the hill, hee had raised brestworkes in which his cannon and great store of small shott was placed; on either fflanke hee was strengthned with a thicke wood which

stood upon the declining of the hill, in which hee had putt store of muskeiteires; on his reare hee had a faire plaine where stood rang'd his reserues of horse and ffootte; some bodyes of horse with muskeiteires hee bestow'd upon some other places of the hill, where hee thought there was any accesse; thus fortyfied stood the foxe gazing at us when our whole Army was raung'd in order of battle upon the large corne field neare Tughill. In this posture wee continued about two houres; nothing passing but loose skirmishes upon Tughill, betwixt a party of our vantgard and a party of horse and dragoones of the enemys sent downe the hill for that purpose. The Kings Army found that the Rebells would not bee drawne to fight but vpon extreame aduantages; and therefore faced about and marched towardes . . .

Other accounts of battles and campaigns are more polemical. They include newsletters, propaganda tracts and broadsheets. The lengthy titles are often themselves evocative of the time and indicative of the bias to follow. Many of these tracts have been published by record societies, and others exist in the original in local libraries and can be reproduced photographically to provide vivid teaching material, especially for secondary-school children. Those teachers able to visit the British (Museum) Library will often find good examples for their locality among the Thomason Tracts. Sometimes records of the armies themselves exist, like the accounts of the Roundhead garrison at Chalfield (Wiltshire), of which the following is an extract.[18]

1645		£	s	d
19 April	Paid to a spy towardes Bathe	0	2	6
	Paid for worm-wood beer	0	1	6
25 April	Paid a messenger to Devizes for intelligence	0	3	0
	Paid the woman that tendes the sick men	0	2	6
	Paid Ancient Moyle to buy butter and eggs	0	3	6
3 May	Paid the Lt. Col. for a week's pay for the post	15	0	0
	Paid Mrs. Eyres for the entertainment of 4 men that came for solders	0	4	0

This sort of material can form the basis not only of imaginative work but of a general investigation of the maintenance of the forces of the two sides, their equipment and activities, maybe as an introduction to a detailed study of the military events of the war. Fieldwork on the sites of local battlegrounds, visits to churches, castles and great houses that were damaged or played a part in the local conflict can profitably be incorporated into syllabuses.

The viciousness of contemporary warfare was more obvious on the

continent than in the English Civil War, but those excesses which did
occur are usually well documented, as, for example, the judgement
of the court martial on the Earl of Derby and his officers in 1651 for
the atrocities they had perpetrated in the war:[19]

> the said Earle to bee beheaded att Bolton in Lancashire that day ffort-
> night; afterwards Captyn Benbowe to bee shott at Shrowesbury the
> same daye; and Sir Tymothy [Featherstonehaught] to bee beheaded att
> Chester that daye three weekes, which was all p'formed accordinglie.
> The nexte weeke afterwards John Saer, Captn John Benbow, and some
> others weire alsoe tryed by a Councell of Warr att Chester and weire
> adiudged to dye. John Saer was hanged vpon the Comon Gallowes att
> Chester on Tuesdaye the ffourth of November; where some more weire
> hanged for seu'all offences the same daye beinge condemned att the
> assizes att Chester held on the weeke before . . .

The Civil War is then a good example of a period where there is
often much vivid local material, attractive to children, available to
illustrate themes usually taught. For older children these sources can
provide the basis for ambitious work, and they can sometimes fire the
imagination of school leavers. Recently eighty senior pupils of a
Tiverton (Devon) school included in a local study a dramatic
representation of events in the area during the Civil War, which was
filmed by Exeter University. The minute books of most town
councils will usually provide some information on the effects on the
daily life of the citizens of the subsequent period of Puritan rule. For
High Wycombe (Buckinghamshire) in 1649, for example there is
record of the oath of loyalty to the Crown previously sworn by
Aldermen, replaced by:[20]

> Yow shall sweare that yow shall be true and faithfull to the Common-
> wealth of England as it is nowe established without kinge or house of
> lords. Yow shall well and truely execute the office and place of an
> Alderman within this Burrough and be aidinge and assistinge att all
> tymes unto the Mayor of this said Burrough for the tyme beinge in all
> lawfull wayes and meanes according to youre best skille knowledge and
> power Soe helpe yow God.

In the next century the emergence and growth of Methodism,
again a subject often taught in the secondary school, can often be
illustrated with lively local examples from the journals of Charles and
John Wesley and from John's letters (published in various editions).
Bishops' visitation returns often throw light on the extent of dissent
and Anglican attitudes to it. The incumbent of Almondsbury

(Yorkshire) for example, noted in 1764 that in his parish of 1,800 families[21]

> We have I think about half a Score Families of Dissenters of which number six I think are Quakers and the rest independents the Methodists I am told are pretty numerous in the Remoter parts of this parish but they are such a Vagrant Sect that it is Impossible to Give any Account of them and besides they will not allow themselves to be called Dissenters.

In the mid-nineteenth century the pattern and extent of church attendance can be illustrated for any part of the country, for in 1851 the only national religious census was carried out. Its findings were published as a parliamentary paper, which can provide total attendances at services on census Sunday for each denomination in each census district.[22] Copies of the original returns from each chapel or church are obtainable from the Public Record Office. Thus at Brunswick Wesleyan Chapel, Leeds, it is recorded that 1,099 attended morning service, including 242 Sunday school children, and 859 attended evening service. There were 700 free seats and 1,582 others, and it was returned that attendance had been reduced by the weather —a showery morning and a stormy evening, with thunder.

A useful exercise for older pupils is the compilation of a present-day survey of local church attendance to compare with attendance locally in 1851.[23] There is scope too, for using directories and maps to plot the whereabouts of places of worship in the past, and for fieldwork in examining buildings which still exist (see Chapter 8). The flavour of past church and chapel life may be all the better recreated by the judicious use of photographs and parish magazines, and the collection from elderly folk of reminiscences of church-going in their parents' times.

For the eighteenth, nineteenth and twentieth centuries there is also much readily available contemporary teaching material to illustrate political events at a local level. Most towns of any size had local newspapers, and often there was both a Whig/Liberal paper and a Tory/Conservative one. All the important issues of the day would be commented on from a national as well as a local point of view. Thus the career of John Wilkes and the popular support he received in various parts of the country are well brought out in the extract from the *Leeds Mercury* of 24 April 1770:

> At Bradford, the morning was ushered in with ringing of bells, which continued till ten at night, and in the evening were illuminations, and

the following, we hear, was given at the sole expence of Mr. Richard Shackleton, at the Bull's Head, viz. A bonefire of 45 loads of coals, a curious representation of the figures 45, composed of 45 candles, under which was wrote, in large characters, *Wilkes at Liberty*; also a supper to the sons of liberty, which consisted of 45 lb. of roast beef; legs of mutton and tongues 45 lb.; three hams 45 lb.; 45 fowls; a lamb 45 lb.; 45 lb. of bread; 45 lb. of vegetables; 45 gallons of ale and 45 bowls of punch; after supper all the loyal healths were drunk

It will be worth searching local newspapers for elections, and for any periods of serious political agitation or unrest[24]—as not only over the Wilkes case but also, for example, for the parliamentary reform Bills, Chartism,[25] the Anti-Corn Law League, the 1870 Education Act, tariff reform, women's suffrage, and popular unrest and labour movements—as well as for aspects of other important phases of national life, like life on the home front during the two world wars. Often local reference libraries will have classified indexes or books of cuttings. Sometimes extracts from newspapers will have been published by local record societies. For municipal, parliamentary and other elections local reference libraries are also likely to have pamphlet and broadsheet material; sometimes local record offices will have agents' and candidates' accounts. Much national legislation had to be effected by local government, and the printed reports of council meetings and of committees and officials, too numerous to describe here, contain a wealth of material. The report of the Royal Commission into Municipal Corporations of the 1830s (a parliamentary paper) includes not only detailed information on aspects of the local government of nearly 300 boroughs, useful when dealing with the Municipal Corporations Act, but comment, too, on the parliamentary franchise. For elections up to 1868 there may be poll books,[26] which not only name all the voters and show how they cast their vote but indicate the sort of persons who enjoyed the franchise. Much information on local variations in representation and franchise is to be found in E. Porritt's *The Unreformed House of Commons* (Cambridge, 1909).

Such topics are on the whole most suitable for older secondary-school pupils, and those following more academic courses. The value of local material in bringing alive what many textbooks continue to make unnecessarily boring is already recognized in the number of teaching kits produced on local elections. One grammar-school history club was sufficiently fired by such material to produce a semi-dramatic tape recording of the Hampshire election of 1790, making use not only of national materials but of evidence found in local newspapers and record offices.[27] It is easy to see how variations of this, such as composite booklets and wall displays, could be undertaken as class exercises which would illuminate understanding of the national as well as the local scene. In larger towns local libraries may well be able to co-operate with teachers in providing for loan or as exhibitions materials concerned with twentieth-century local politics— such as the movement for women's suffrage, co-operatives and trade unions, and also life on the home front in the two wars, and during the period 1919–39. Some material may also be collected from pupils' homes—such as photographs and relics like identity cards, ration books and so on. The oral reminiscences of local inhabitants, too, can fruitfully be tapped. Indeed, the volume of easily accessible original materials available locally to illustrate aspects of modern political and general history is out of all proportion to the space devoted to it here.[28] The past activities of local government may often be illustrated also by the field study of streets, buildings and estates.

Schools and schooling

The history of education, and particularly the growth of State control and the effects of national legislation on schooling, is a topic which can readily be illustrated from local records, often from those relating to schools known to the pupil.[29] The study of local school life in the past—as 'our school in Victorian times'—can also be used as a basis for a branching out into a general study of national and local social conditions. Although there are records on education for the periods before the eighteenth century they are not on the whole very suitable for use in teaching. Some secondary schools which originated as endowed grammar schools may well have their own published histories,[30] and the *Victoria County History* also has histories of such schools. The centenary of the Education Act of 1870 resulted in many local histories of schooling, most with interesting photographs and illustrations, and local libraries will know of these.

For the grammar schools interesting source material is readily available in print from the early nineteenth century. Nicholas Carlisle's *Concise Description of the Endowed Grammar Schools in England and Wales* (1818; Richmond, 1972) prints much information on the state of many schools in 1818. Many entries are long and detailed. The following for Thursby (Cumberland) is a short one and is an example of a grammar school which had become partly an elementary school:

The School-house at Thursby was built by the principal Inhabitants of this Township, by Subscription, about Eighty years ago. There is no original Endowment. But, about the year 1802, Mr. Thomas Thomlinson, of Newbury, in North Carolina, Merchant, and a Native of Thursby left, by his Will bearing date in 1798, the sum of £354. to this School; which is now lent on interest to Sir Wastell Brisco, Bart., of Crofton Hall, for the use of the Master . . . The School is open to all the Children of the Parishoners and others, on their paying a small Quarter-pence. There are usually from 40 to 50 Boys and Girls in the Winter and Spring; and from 30 to 40 in the Summer and Autumn. Ward's Latin and Greek Grammars are used: but very few are taught the Classics; the Education in general being reading, writing, and arithmetic. The present Master is, The Revd. John Mason, whose emoluments are about £25. *per annum.* He is also Curate of the Parish.

Nineteenth-century parliamentary papers provide a great deal on grammar and other secondary schools. There are the reports of the Charity Commission of the early nineteenth century, of the Taunton Commission (1868–9), and of the Bryce Commission of 1895. The following report on a grammar school in Beccles (Suffolk) for 1867 from the Taunton report is excellent for a class exercise, for it compresses into a short space so much information, and can be used, for example, to draw up comparisons of school life then and now, or for exercises in historical imagination.

General Character—Classical. In age of scholars, second grade.

Masters—Head master a clergyman, M.A. of Cambridge, late Fellow of Magdalene College, receives from endowment £193, besides fees for instruction and profits of boarders. Second master, and masters for extra subjects, appointed and paid by head master.

Day Scholars—Nineteen (in 1864 ten), chiefly between 10 and 14 years old, chiefly sons of professional men and tradesmen, all from within one mile of school. Pay £10 10s. for general work. German, £6 6s. Drawing, £4 4s. Stationery, 10s. Do not attend on Sunday.

Boarders—Thirty-three (in 1864 twenty-two), all in head master's house. Three or four meals a day; meat once. Terms for board and instruction, according to age, 50 to 60 guineas. Laundress, £2 2s. Private study, £4 4s., or £2 2s. if shared with another boy. School bills: highest £80; average, £63; lowest, £54. Cubical contents of bedrooms, 504 feet per boy. Hours, 7½ a.m., 8½ to 9½ p.m.

Instruction, Discipline, etc.—Boys on admission must be able to begin Latin. School classified by classics and mathematics chiefly, and other subjects subordinately. School course modified to suit particular cases. Religious instruction in Greek Testament and Paley's *Evidences.* School opened and, except on half holidays, closed with prayers.

Promotion partly by half year's work and partly by monthly examinations, and separate for each group of subjects. Examination once a month by master. Prizes distributed after general examination at Midsummer.

Punishments: impositions, detention, confinement to school or playground, and caning; last not much resorted to, but generally inflicted in presence of the whole school.

Playground about two acres. Boys, except seniors, not allowed to leave school premises without permission.

Five boys have gone to university within last five years.

School time, 38 or 39 weeks per annum. Study, 29 hours per week, besides time for writing exercises and preparation of all lessons except construing. Playtime, 28 or 30 hours per week.

For the growth of elementary education it is usually possible to find good teaching material for Sunday schools, charity schools, church and chapel schools (voluntary schools), private schools, board schools, and council schools. Again there are parliamentary papers, especially reports for 1818 and 1833 which list existing schools for each town or parish.[31] The following extract from the 1833 report for one of the three parishes of the borough of Hertford could again be used as a lead into a study of the provision of education at that time.

ANDREW'S, ST., WITHIN AND WITHOUT, Parish (Pop. 2,120) *One Infant School*, wherein 9 males and 10 females are receiving instruction at the expense of their parents.—*Ten Daily Schools*: two whereof are *National* Schools, in one of which are 161 males, and in the other are 45 females, of whom 40 are clothed; another contains 45 females; the three Schools above described are supported by voluntary contributions: two other Schools (commenced 1822) contain respectively 50 males, and 4 males and 28 females: in two others (commenced 1828) are 8 males and 29 females; in another (commenced 1830) are 17 males and 8 females; in another (commenced 1832) are 14 males and 20 females; and in the other (commenced 1833) are 2 males and 14 females: in the seven Schools last-mentioned the instruction is wholly at the expense of their parents—*One Evening School* (commenced 1822) at which are 40 females, whose instruction is paid for by their parents.—*Three Sunday Schools*, supported by voluntary contributions: in one of which (commenced 1827) are 20 females, who attend the Established Church, another, consisting of 50 males and 70 females, appertains to Independent Dissenters; and the other, of 24 males and 32 females, to the Baptist denomination.

A much more detailed investigation published as a parliamentary paper (1852-3, xc)—the education census for 1851—provides even better material for similar exercises. There is scope in such sources, used in conjunction with more recent guides and directories and census figures, to make comparative maps or tables showing the spread of schools in an area, perhaps comparing the situation in the mid-nineteenth century with that today. Photographs of school buildings that have disappeared and field visits to remaining buildings can give material for illustrated descriptions of changing types of school building.[32]

Later in the century the reports of the Newcastle Commission and of the Cross Commission give full information on some parts of the country for a period a decade before the Elementary Education Act of 1870 and fifteen or so years after. There are also many other parliamentary papers which might be consulted, and though most cannot find mention here[33] it may be noted that for some areas reports of factory and mines inspectors and official reports on the employment of women and children in industry and agriculture often provide very colourful material. Interesting, too, are the Registrar General's annual reports (parliamentary papers from 1839), which show by counties (and for 1859–84 by census districts) the number of brides and grooms unable to sign their names on marriage. Thus for Cornwall for 1865 we have:

| District | No. of marriages | Those unable to sign name on marriage | | |
		Grooms	Brides	Total
Stratton	41	7	11	18
Camelford	55	19	22	41
Launceston	105	25	29	54
St Germans	70	10	13	23
Liskeard	241	73	100	173
Bodmin	146	32	38	70
St Columb	133	39	44	83
St Austell	250	80	111	191
Truro	371	106	121	227
Falmouth	199	32	45	77
Helston	246	91	102	193
Redruth	573	214	286	500
Penzance	527	170	220	390
Scilly Isles	24	2	3	5

Clearly there is scope for work here for secondary pupils and older juniors to calculate total numbers marrying, percentages of male and female illiterates in each place, and perhaps taking a report ten or more years later and comparing the differences. Comparison with some other part of the country can also be undertaken, and perhaps the relationship between illiteracy and heavily populated mining and industrial districts investigated. Sometimes it will be possible, using such sources as the 1851 education census, to relate the school attendance then to later literacy levels.

It is likely, however, that there will be plenty of examples of the records of individual schools available locally, maybe even of the school the children are attending. Particularly interesting are school registers, timetables, punishment books and pupil teachers' record books. Log books, too, are very useful. These were journals kept from the 1840s or before by head teachers which include details of attendance, the curriculum, attainments of children, references to assistant and pupil teachers, copies of inspectors' reports,[34] and evidence on relations with school inspectors and managers. A good log book is sufficient in itself to form the basis for a junior-school class to study the development of education during the last century or more.[35] There is clearly scope for project work, drama, imaginative writing and drawing, and modelling. Subjects for investigation can include the curriculum, the buildings, the teachers and children, holidays, attendance figures, visitors and inspectors, school discipline and so on. Information on outbreaks of infectious diseases, ages of children, occupations of parents, and jobs to which children went can be found from log books. School registers may give an indication of the topographical area from which the pupils were drawn, their ages at entry and leaving, reasons for leaving school, occupations of parents, and so forth. In more recent times school magazines will provide much information for secondary schools, and for all types of schools the recollections of local adults may be of interest. The local archive office may have the records of the school boards and the local education authorities, and though many of these will not be of value for teaching purposes, some may be, as, for example, plans of school buildings, photographs, school attendance officers' records, and school board election posters and annual reports.

Sometimes schools, record offices or the children's own homes will provide exercise books from the past, and these can cause great interest. An essay like the following on 'Boys' written by a thirteen-year-old girl in 1897 can clearly lead to all sorts of interesting work:[36]

> I do not like boys. They are so rough and noisy. They think themselves much cleverer than girls but they are mistaken. Girls are much more useful to their mothers than boys. If you see a boy nursing a baby, he does it so clumsily you think all the time he is going to let it drop. Boys

make their sisters do all sorts of things, such as clean their boots, brush their clothes, put their playthings—bats, balls, and marbles safely away. When a boy has tooth-ache he makes a deal more fuss about it than a girl would, and mother has to do a deal of things to make him quiet. Then boys are so fond of play that they cannot find time to come for their meals, and if they are not ready just when they want they make a row about it. The best thing to do then is to let them go without, and you may be sure that they will come to the bread and butter, before the bread and butter will go to them. It costs more to keep boys than girls, they wear out their boots so quickly and tear their clothes so dreadfully that the shoemaker and tailor are always calling at the house. Girls do not wear out half so many clothes. Folks say girls talk more than boys, but you should hear them at ball or marbles and then you would not think so. Well, I suppose there must be boys or we should have no one to build houses, shoe horses, plough the fields, look after gardens and shops. The nicest boy I know is Willie Murphy, he is a very nice fellow.

Public health and living conditions

For early modern times many of the records described elsewhere may be used to illustrate local living conditions. The seventeenth-century hearth tax returns indicate the relative proportion of larger and smaller dwellings in a community, and probate inventories, as we have seen, can help a pupil to visualize each room in a house of the period. Borough council minutes from the sixteenth century on contain telling references to street cleaning and sanitary regulations, water supply, and disease. The *Calendar of State Papers, Domestic* for Tudor and Stuart times is full of references to 'plague' (the eclectic term applied to several types of epidemic disease) and its effects in many parts of the country, such as the following letter of 1665 to Samuel Pepys, an example of the colourful material available for class use:

It is too true that the plague is at Newport [Isle of Wight], brought over by a certain knight who had an estate there, and sickened and died at his lodgings; the master of the house thought it quinsy, and threatened the mayor for shutting up the house, but two women took the infection and died from merely changing and airing the sheets of his bed; the poor gentleman was obliged to bury the bodies himself in his own garden; sheep and goats since put in the house are all dead; the plague increases at Southampton.

For the larger towns there are often other miscellaneous records concerning epidemics,[37] and burial registers for both early modern

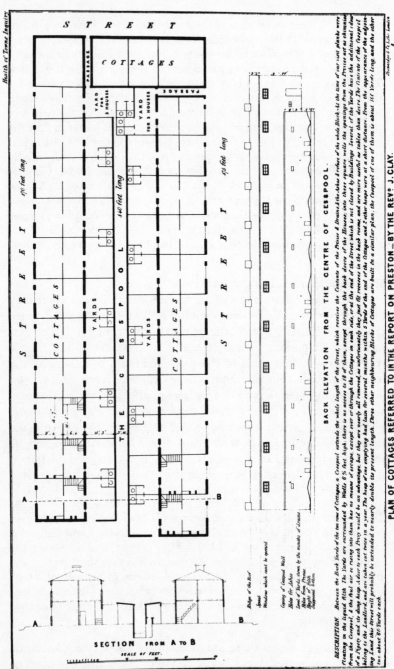

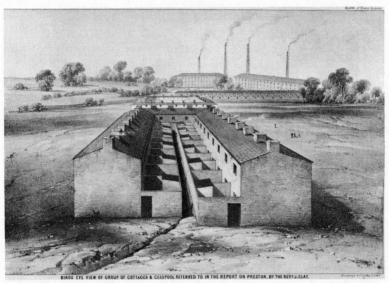

BIRDS EYE VIEW OF GROUP OF COTTAGES & CESSPOOL REFERRED TO IN THE REPORT ON PRESTON..BY THE REV? J.CLAY.

4 (*opposite page*) Plan of cottages referred to in the report on Preston, from the first report of the Commissioners for Inquiry into the State of Large Towns and Populous Districts, 1844 (British Parliamentary Paper, Session 1844, vol. xvii), appendix to the report, between pp. 34–5
5 (*above*) Bird's-eye view of the group of cottages and cesspool referred to in the report on Preston, from *ibid*.
6 (*below*) The bird's-eye view as redrawn by a sixth-form pupil

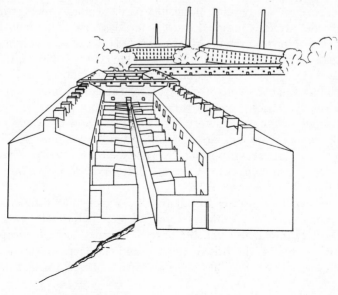

times and later can also illustrate the effects of epidemics, as well as common ages of death, and sometimes causes, and the extent of infant mortality. But it is the nineteenth century which commonly provides the most interesting and detailed original local sources suitable for use with children of all ages. Records relating to poor relief, especially the reports of boards of guardians after 1834, official reports on the employment of women and children in agriculture, local newspapers, guidebooks and directories contain much on public health, housing and living conditions. The published censuses provide information on housing densities and the age structure of inhabitants of localities. From 1839 we have the annual reports of the Registrar General (see last section), which contain not only a great deal of statistical material on deaths and their causes but also vivid reports on general public health matters in various places. The following is from the report for 1866:

> Besides coal smoke there are in . . . Manchester various solid impuri-
> ties to which persons who live in the country are less exposed. The
> houses stand close to the roads or street . . . and from these streets . . .
> a fine impalpable dust is continually thrown up by the great and incessant
> traffic of drays and carriages of all types . . . to the residents they must
> be a constant source of bronchial irritation . . . In the cleaning of cotton
> or of woollen rags, a vast amount of dust is given off . . . In the fustian-
> cutting rooms there is a constant fine filamentous dust . . .

There are many other published parliamentary papers which can provide attractive original sources for class use. Especially fruitful are the reports on the health of towns (1840), the state of large towns (1844-5), and the housing of the working classes (1884-5), but there are many others. The report of the General Board of Health on Cholera Epidemics, 1848-9 (1850), for example, contains reports on individual places. Some of these parliamentary papers contain such material as graphs of mortality, and plans and drawings of slum housing and sanitary arrangements. The illustrations for Preston (figs. 4-6) are taken from the *Report on the State of Large Towns*, and opposite is an extract for Clerkenwell from the *Report on the Housing of the Working Classes* of 1885.

An invaluable source for many places exists in local reports to the General Board of Health, of which 398 were published between 1848 and 1857. Some are available in local libraries, and photocopies are obtainable from the British Library and the Department of Health and Social Security. They cover all aspects of local public health and

Deaths in Clerkenwell from chief zymotic diseases, 1874–83

	Small-pox	Measles	Scarlet fever	Whooping cough	Typhus	Diar-rhoea	Total
1874	2	63	71	38	31	55	260
1875	2	36	76	82	24	58	278
1876	2	48	34	41	12	73	210
1877	15	73	82	36	25	53	284
1878	1	39	41	56	25	73	235
1879	1	74	44	61	11	36	227
1880	2	26	51	87	14	65	245
1881	10	39	54	53	26	58	240
1882	0	61	60	81	18	40	260
1883	0	61	46	33	16	59	215

It is really monstrous to compare the mortality of the most densely massed, if not overcrowded, central districts [of London], especially when, as the School Board inspector says, over 30 per cent of the parents are out of work, 40 per cent of the poor children came to school without a breakfast, and 40 per cent without a dinner, with that of the sparse and scattered population of other districts of the metropolis. In this Clerkenwell, with its 180 persons per acre, has to compete with Kensington with its 78, and Marylebone (Cavendish Square) with its 103 per acre . . .

include plans, maps and statistics as well as detailed descriptions and evidence.[38] Local record offices or local government departments may possess interesting maps and plans relating to housing and public health.[39] Especially good if they exist are the large-scale local health maps which the General Board encouraged local boards to produce, and which are useful for illustrating building densities, water supply, sewerage and so on. For many towns for the latter part of the century there will exist in the council records annual reports from the medical officer of health, usually printed and brimful of information interesting to children. In directories there may be details of hospitals and infirmaries, and sometimes the domestic records of such institutions—rules and regulations, diet sheets and so forth—may exist locally.

The opportunity such records provide for imaginative work, literary and dramatic, for map making, for the construction of graphs and models, and for project work, is very obvious. Those teaching various age groups will find much, too, to provide illustration of oral explanations, for expansion of textbook descriptions, for the basis of work cards, for a lead-in to all sorts of aspects of history and social studies, and sometimes for urban fieldwork.[40] For pupils following social, local or environmental studies there is much relevant historical background material for comparison with present-day conditions.[41]

For notes to this chapter see pp. 170–2.

8 Fieldwork and archaeology

Unlike many aspects of history, local history requires the physical study of the landscape and of the visible evidence of man's activity, for although written evidence is as essential as for other aspects of history much more evidence than the documentary is available for the study of almost any locality. Moreover for some aspects of local history physical evidence is either the only or the prime evidence of the past.

General considerations and planning

In school, fieldwork adds to the variety of approaches and activities which local studies offer, and, particularly with pupils below the sixth form, the learning process is assisted when visible and tangible evidence is added to the written word and to the teacher's oral explanations. Moreover the study of such evidence takes place in different, often interesting and therefore more memorable surroundings. And extra-mural activities help to break the barrier between the classroom, which to many pupils seems artificial and remote from their 'real' existence, and the outside world of streets, fields and ordinary people. Topics studied from literary material become more meaningful when their physical setting is investigated. Thus early canals can be studied from books, maps, illustrations and records with enjoyment, interest and appreciation; but to see a lock in operation and to walk along a bridle path makes for fuller comprehension.

Again the experience of children both generally and in relation to historical and allied studies is broadened by contact with places, situations and people not part of school life yet also not part of the world of office, factory and shop which makes up the working life of so many adults. Fieldwork has a special value in schools in new towns or serving new estates which appear to have little history and whose inhabitants perhaps have less interest in the local past than those who live in older towns or suburbs where visible evidence is plentiful. Children can be brought into contact with sites and buildings of interest in the proximity so that they begin to think of themselves as belonging to a larger area and an older community. Fieldwork also illustrates to pupils the fact that history is all around them, that there are adults other than teachers involved in revealing and recording the past. They become aware of and learn to appreciate that this involves skills other than the ability to dip into books and remember facts.

Fieldwork is also valuable for the contact it brings between subject areas. Outside the classroom the pupil is confronted with an amalgam of evidence pertaining to many of the aspects of academic study, which in school are more easily attacked individually. The same environment is used by the geographer, the geologist, the biologist and the social scientist as by the local historian. Historical fieldwork can demonstrate the links between certain aspects of history and those of other disciplines. The local environment is thus particularly suitable as a basis for interdisciplinary or combined studies, and few teaching local or environmental studies would be rash enough to ignore completely the physical existence of the past in the present. Geographers must be credited with an earlier appreciation of the environment as a teaching medium than historians. Although the use of fieldwork to introduce historical geography is only just beginning, the interrelationship of history, geology and geography in such matters as the siting of settlements, the development of communications, types of industry and agriculture, and so on has long been accepted.[1] And wherever the teacher of local history uses the 'then and now' comparative approach his 'now' is also the geographer's and social scientist's field. The link with biology is less well forged but is becoming more important, for such matters as flora and fauna cannot be totally ignored, and in some respects biologists can provide important evidence for the historian. In the lower forms of junior schools the study of the environment can involve an even wider spectrum of subjects. Mathematical skills can be practised—in measuring, counting, and making plans, graphs and tables; art and craft and other practical work can be brought in for recording and follow-up activities; and, for English, comparative, imaginative work and drama can also be inspired by fieldwork.

The skills of accurate observation and recording can be encouraged from an early age through fieldwork, and, particularly for older children, other interests and skills are often fostered too. Interest in architecture, geology and nature study, in sketching, photography, walking, cycling, climbing, are often stimulated. For children whose homes do not provide contact with the countryside this can be of extreme significance for, as R. S. Peters has put it, 'to be educated . . . is to travel with a different view'. With encouragement, fieldwork undifferentiated by subject may assume a peculiar value for the unacademic school leavers, whose interests lie largely outside the walls of school and the pages of books.[2] Thus surveys of the areas in which they live, of the industries in which they will work, and the problems of the communities they will be adult members of, none of which can be understood without historical as well as other perspectives, may well touch off the spark of curiosity and awaken the feeling of belonging so necessary for a full life.[3]

Fieldwork, indeed, offers much for children of all ages and abilities.[4] The combination of work outside and inside the classroom leads to an enormous variety of individual activity, practical and more academic, eminently suitable for group work and for work with mixed-ability classes. As well as serving social and environmental studies, it can enrich the study of local history in its own right and provide depth to the study of national history. A visit to a monastery or a castle can, for example, be used to illustrate general aspects of religious and military life in the Middle Ages, or the special significance of the presence of a particular abbey or castle in the history of the locality. For those who would study the local history of another area for comparative purposes fieldwork based on a residential centre can, of course, be particularly useful.[5] In fieldwork, with its emphasis on personal experience and activity, a very real understanding of the local environment may be engendered: and a sound knowledge of this is a necessary basis of appreciating wider issues and affairs.

There are, of course, difficulties involved in incorporating field-work in syllabuses. In secondary schools complex timetable arrangements may be a hindrance, especially if the provision of an appropriate staff–pupil ratio for outdoor work can be achieved only by disrupting normal lessons. Sometimes the involvement of student teachers or even parents may help here, and sometimes weekends and holiday periods can be utilized. Another inhibiting factor is that of expense, and here history fieldwork has yet to obtain the general recognition of need at last accepted for biology and geography. Meanwhile parents and general school funds will often need to be called on. This is particularly unfortunate in downtown schools, where such backing is weak, but it should not inhibit the teacher from using fieldwork. The environment starts at the school gate or even in the school grounds, and much can be undertaken by excursions on foot or short bus journeys.[6] Fieldwork is not less fieldwork because it is conducted within the time span of a single period or afternoon; and such expeditions can often be augmented by larger and more protracted ones, perhaps once a term if that is all that can be afforded. Fortunately there is increasing appreciation of outdoor work, and there has been a growth of residential study centres, camp schools and school outposts. In addition there are the Youth Hostels and residential centres run by the Field Studies Council, and a Council for Urban Studies has been formed.[7]

There are some dangers, too. Geographers, for example, use the technique of 'then and now' in a historical approach to their subject, and this approach is used by history teachers too, both in the classroom and in fieldwork. It must be remembered, however, that while there may be only one 'now' there is an infinite number of 'thens', and care must be taken in using this technique to be sure children appreciate the periods they are considering and the nature of stages of development and change. Another danger, most apparent when fieldwork is used only infrequently, is that the trip becomes not part of 'work' but merely a sort of Sunday-school treat. Of course, enjoyment of this kind is not taboo but essentially fieldwork is work and should be recognized as such. It has been said that there are 'few sadder sights in education than that of children wandering aimlessly in an area of rich historic interest'.[8] The level of triviality to which unplanned and unstructured activities can descend and the frailty of the intellectual basis of such an approach have been rightly castigated by Professor Bantock.[9]

In fact fieldwork should form part of the normal curriculum, whether that be history or some form of integrated studies, and should complement what is undertaken in the classroom. It can thus be a recurring element in a series of lessons, the climax to the study of a topic, or an introduction to further study. In any event it requires careful planning and preparation as part of the overall syllabus.

Planning of a special nature is needed, too. The success of any expedition, however brief, depends on careful logistical preparation. Attention to such matters as organization of timetables, transport, meals, insurance, information for parents, first-aid preparations, behaviour and discipline, is essential—but is not peculiar to history, and there is not sufficient space to deal with it here.[10] In addition the teacher must familiarize himself with the fieldwork the locality offers, and see that the school possesses the necessary resources for it to be undertaken.

There are a number of good introductions to fieldwork generally and its place in teaching, and for some areas regional guides exist to assist the teacher.[11] The history teacher should also become thoroughly familiar with any places (including sites and museums) he intends to use, both through books and by preliminary visits on his own, to decide what aspects are most suitable to stress with particular age groups, and to note purely practical matters such as the length of time likely to be spent at different stages. Visits by pupils to sites unfamiliar to their teachers are unlikely to be profitable. The school library should be stocked with relevant works, including as many guides to local sites and buildings as possible, and local OS maps, especially the 1 in. but also, particularly for towns, those of larger scale, and photographs where relevant. The history room should have plenty of boards for clipping papers and maps to for work in the open and also plastic map cases. If possible models, slides or large-scale pictures and photographs of places often visited should be available for preliminary work.

Classroom preparation of pupils both generally and for specific expeditions is essential. Older children should, for example, be thoroughly familiar with how to orientate maps, read map symbols, interpret scales, read and make map references, and use compasses. Often preliminary work in and about the school grounds will be helpful. Younger children will need special assistance in the understanding of two-dimensional cartographic representation and scale, and it will usually be found best to provide simplified plans instead of or as well as detailed maps. They will need instruction, too, in the techniques of recording, by means of sketches and notes. Older pupils may wish to use cameras and tape recorders, and again preliminary guidance will be needed. Before any particular visit is undertaken, preparatory work specific to that expedition will be needed. The teacher should make sure that pupils understand how the visits fit into the syllabus. Buildings or sites should be studied from maps, guidebooks and plans, and if possible from photographs and models, too. Models can sometimes be borrowed from school museum services; or they may be the fruit of former pupils' work. If museums or stately homes are being visited pupils must be told which parts are to be seen and what the important exhibits are.

Then there must be no doubt as to what work the pupils are required to undertake in the field. Work can be assigned to groups, pairs or individuals according to the interests, abilities and needs of the children concerned. Group or pair work has the advantage of providing companionship and fostering co-operation, but each child should be provided with a written indication of what he has to do. This may well take the form of an assignment sheet or booklet, which should, where appropriate, be prefaced by a plan of the site or build-ing, a sketch map showing its geographical position in relation to the school or town, and a summary of basic information. Assignments should not consist of random 'quiz' questions requiring one-word answers but be devised to provide, when completed, a body of useful and connected information, preferably requiring not only written notes but sketches too. Work cards may include base maps or plans to which more information may be added, or sketches (as, for instance, of architectural features) examples of which are to be found on the site. On the whole it is preferable, where a place of any complexity is being visited, for different groups of pupils to be assigned to study different aspects of the building or site. Thus in a visit to a town one group may make a special study of churches and chapels, one pair within the group may concentrate on noting the denominations involved, another on the age and external architecture, another on internal features. Other groups may study public buildings, dwelling houses, shops, streets, and so on.

In a visit to a great house some pupils may be assigned to collect information, written and graphic, on the furniture, others on the paintings and the tapestries, others on aspects of architectural style, and others on china and ornaments. Some may be set to study the dimensions and nature of different types of room and their contents; others to collect evidence on the servants' quarters and to deduce the work servants would have had to undertake. In a projected visit to a castle some children might be required to pay special attention to the defensive arrangements, others to concern themselves with the architecture and building materials, with water supply, sanitation and so forth. For all such activities the appropriate materials will need to be provided—paper, crayons, felt pens, portable tape recorders, compasses, binoculars, cameras, measuring equipment, etc—and within groups it may be necessary to allocate the types of recording to be undertaken. For example, one or two children might be responsible for measuring, one for photography, another for sketching and another for identifying examples. Or a group responsible for making sketches of a building might divide the recording into those who draw plans, those who sketch side elevations, those who copy details of architectural style, those responsible for certain parts of the building, such as the gatehouse, and so on.

Teachers should exploit the potential of local museums, general and specialized, which inevitably contain materials relating to the history of the area.[12] Some have special teachers or instructors attached to them; most have a member of staff able to give a short talk on certain topics. Some museums produce booklets or duplicated 'hand-outs' for children, and all will be willing to give advice on suitable objects in their possession or in the locality generally. School museum services often lend visual aids, models and original objects.[13] Class visits should be frequent for specific purposes, linked to what is being learnt in school and preferably planned in conjunction with the museum authorities. Pupils should also be encouraged to use museums on their own, too, just as they use the local library. Local museums often contain finds from historic sites in the vicinity, so that visits to museums should be combined (not necessarily on the same day) with visits to the sites.

In the field the history teacher's duties are not, of course, to be confined to supervision. Though a guided lecture tour should be avoided, there is usually a place for an oral exposition to the class as a whole, by the teacher or a guide, and opportunity should be given for group discussions. Teachers must also assist individuals and groups pursuing their assignments, and much more is likely to be learnt from the teacher's spontaneous conversation in the course of the work than by listening to a prepared talk delivered to a large group.

Surveys, urban and rural

General investigations, or surveys, of a place or an area, rural or urban, looking at developments over a period of time, and perhaps contrasting the past with the present, are useful in the study of local history in its own right and in environmental studies, social studies and integrated history–geography.[14] These must, of course, embrace not only fieldwork but also the use of written evidence in the class-room, and are particularly valuable for demonstrating the inter-relationship of the different facets of the make-up of a community, such as population, local government, religion, industry, communications. The general advantages of fieldwork in strengthening the bonds between school work and the outside world are, therefore, especially strong in survey work, with its concern with a wide spectrum of the physical environment.

There are, however, potential drawbacks in using surveys. First, if too ambitious they will absorb time and energy in quantities disproportionate to their pedagogic importance. Secondly, too much survey work presently undertaken in schools is rather trivial in its nature and of doubtful educational value. A little dispassionate appraisal is therefore required in planning and carrying out surveys, which if well done can be so rewarding. Often it is desirable to determine fairly firm topographical limits to the project. With large towns it may be necessary sometimes, especially with younger pupils, to confine attention to one district or the central area. If study of a long chronological period is envisaged a sampling or 'patch' approach should be adopted. The number of topics to be treated will also have to be kept within limits and related to what is useful and interesting to the particular class of children concerned in relation to the time available. For senior secondary pupils and early school leavers it may be possible and appropriate to devote a solid block of time, or the whole time allotted to history, social studies or environmental studies, to making a thorough survey of the whole history of an area. For younger secondary-school pupils the best method may be to carry out a limited survey in each school year, relating it to one or two topics or to one chronological period (to be compared with the present). With older junior-school pupils a fairly wide survey may be undertaken, choosing aspects of the history of a place appropriate to the cognitive abilities and interests of that age group, and limiting to one period in the past (say the late Victorian period or the inter-war years) any comparison with the present.

Basic to field surveys of both rural and urban areas is the comparison of the physical structure and appearance of the area in various times in the past with the present. Initial exercises may thus embrace a study of the geographical structure and its relationship to basic communications; the bringing up to date of the most recent edition of the OS map by the examination on the ground of recent changes; and a comparison of this with the earliest OS map and earlier maps and plans—in all this combining work in the classroom with fieldwork. With younger pupils it may be preferable to provide duplicated sketch maps based upon the OS maps rather than to use the OS maps directly. This sort of work encourages the observation of significant features of urban and rural settlement, and gives a basic topographical and geographical knowledge.

In urban areas surveys may include investigation (using the recording techniques discussed above) of the factors involved in the establishment and growth of the town; its industries and their location; the social and economic structure as evidenced in the physical make-up of different districts—again all in conjunction with work in the classroom. Factors of site location may be demonstrated by initial map work and discussion in school and then by the following of a 'trail' or 'traverse' to examine *in situ* the bridge where there was once a ford and the roads that converge there, the dock that marked the navigable limit of the river, or the abbey, church, castle or market place around which the original town grew up. Another simple trail might illustrate different periods of the town's existence by leading the children to observe successively Roman, medieval, early modern and later buildings and remains. Again, trails might be organized for different groups working outwards from the town centre and noting the different functions and nature of each district, including, for example, the dates of construction of the domestic and other buildings, the types of housing and their likely relationship to social groupings, areas of industrial activity, and so on. Older pupils might be led on to compare the results of this work with such theoretic concepts as concentric models of the city—with its central business zone; a transitional zone of mixed low-grade older residential property, small business and light industry; a zone of cheaper residential houses and flats; a zone of middle-class residences; and surburban and community zones.[15] They may find that different segments or trails reveal somewhat different progressions from the centre, with industry and working-class municipal housing concentrated on one side of a city, or physical and man-made features which have affected the development in a unique fashion. Thus the existence and later enclosure of common land, as at Nottingham, for example, may have affected development, or the earlier existence of walls and gates may have affected road development. An alternative type of trail could deal with this sort of aspect of urban structure by sampling certain parts of a town illustrative of its different aspects, past and present. All this should, of course, go hand-in-hand with the study in class of relevant records such as directories and census material.

Other trails might involve visits to industrial or former industrial districts for observation of their relationship to transport facilities, such as canals, railways and roads, and perhaps bringing out reasons for shifts in industrial locations. Again work in class with such records as directories and maps will provide clues to the location of industries in the past, and provide, for example, material on the size, nature and distribution of retail shops in the past for comparison in the field with the present. Similar trails can be devised for the study of changing architectural styles in domestic, business, civic and industrial architecture; the growth of amenities such as parks, open spaces, shopping centres, places of worship, cinemas, schools, libraries, museums and so on. Domestic architecture alone, taken in relation to social structure, can provide a great deal of work taking in such matters as size, type, building materials, and their relation to the type of occupant and the time of construction.[16]

Just as country children can undertake urban surveys in nearby towns, city children should conduct surveys in the neighbouring countryside. Surveys to investigate the siting and growth of villages are often simpler operations than similar work in towns, and for smaller places the whole village can be included. Physical reasons for the siting of a village and the structure of communications can be deduced from map and photographic work backed up by illustration on the ground, as can identification of the nature of the original settlement. The dating of buildings to indicate the stages of growth can then follow. The demographic, occupational and social history of the village can be discovered from the written evidence discussed elsewhere, but also from physical evidence in the shape of market houses, inns, mills, quarries, mines, and from talking to inhabitants and visiting museums.

In largely agricultural areas farming is an appropriate topic for study. Much can be based on the documentary sources described elsewhere, but since the type of farming is likely to have been at least partly related to the geological and physical structure of the landscape fieldwork will provide additional insight. There is indeed considerable scope for the combination of map work and fieldwork here and in the study of the topography of the place. Older maps, including tithe maps, and more recent maps such as the OS can be compared on the ground to the present physiognomy. Groups of pupils can concentrate each on a different aspect—such as the distribution of farm houses, cottages and outbuildings, the size and type of fields and field boundaries, the roads and lanes, and the existence of woodland, moorland, marsh, village greens and commons. If there is an enclosure or pre-enclosure map it may be possible to show where the old boundaries of the common fields have been retained. In some places traces of ridge-and-furrow and lynchet strips may still be discernible. If areas of strips are well defined older pupils may be given the task of recording the pattern taken by them and their dimensions, relating them to the physical features, in particular the gradient.[17] Sometimes aerial photographs of the area exist, betraying old field systems, and these, like maps, can be used in conjunction with fieldwork. Again pupils can find out whether any of the old roads, footpaths, quarries, parish pounds and so on, described in the enclosure award and swept away by it, are in any way still discernible.[18] In areas of scattered farms and hamlets, when parliamentary enclosure did not take place because the land was already largely enclosed, as, for example, in Devon and parts of Kent, older field and lane patterns found in early maps still exist and can be identified.

The ages of recent hedges can be dated from maps, but for older hedges dating by means of counting the number of different species of trees and shrubs they contain is a developing technique. Tentative results suggest that hedges dating from Saxon times will have nine to twelve different species, those of Tudor origin four, those of a century or less only one—that is, roughly one species for each century.[19] There is opportunity here for interesting group work with children relating geographical, botanical and historical fieldwork.

Some 2,000 sites of villages deserted at various times in the past exist, concentrated in midland and eastern England. They may have left traces in isolated churches, ruined buildings, prominent earthworks, or merely bumps in a field; sometimes aerial photographs revealing the layout are available. For all counties lists can be bought from the Deserted Medieval Village Research Group.[20] The subject is complex and needs careful study by the teacher[21] to familiarize himself with the deserted villages in his area and the reasons for their disappearance as well as the practicalities of the interpretation of physical remains. It would be unwise to embark on investigations with pupils without this preliminary work. Some classroom work, too, will need to precede fieldwork. The children will have to be made familiar with the background, and some preliminary discussion and map work is desirable. On the site a detective approach is often the most fruitful, with children attempting to identify and plot on an outline map the positions of trackways, major buildings, pounds, open fields, villagers' homes and so on, and then discussing their conclusions with the teacher on the spot.[22]

For recent history, surveys may well include contact with older local inhabitants who can provide information from direct experience of periods up to seventy or so years ago, and perhaps recall conversations they had when young with people of earlier generations. Professional historians have now accepted the use of 'oral history' surveys to provide evidence for local and national social history. The value of such material, at a more popular level, in recreating a past society is demonstrated by, for example, Ronald Blythe's *Akenfield*.

Children have always learnt much about the recent past from parents, older relatives and acquaintances, and the merit of incorporating family history into school work is beginning to be appreciated.[23] As well as family contacts, others—clergymen, museum curators, former or practising farmers, craftsmen and factory workers, shopkeepers, soldiers and so on—can all provide detailed information about aspects of local life one or two generations ago. Careful consideration will be needed, however, in organizing contacts between them and pupils. First lists of persons willing and suitable will need to be compiled, and appointments arranged. Sometimes it is worth approaching old persons' homes and clubs. It is desirable to give some prior notice of the topics about which questions will be posed, so that the subject can gather his thoughts and perhaps collect some relevant physical objects, such as photographs, letters, medals, certificates and so on. Pupils and teachers should have agreed on the themes to be covered and the basic questions to be asked. If any sort of statistical work is envisaged, then an interview form may need to be drawn up, and in all events pupils undertaking interviews should be primed to note such vital information as the age of the subject and the chronological period being described. Younger pupils will certainly need duplicated questionnaires which seek brief answers to specific and fairly simple questions; but they should also be encouraged later to recall verbally some of the detailed descriptions they have heard.[24] Both older juniors and secondary pupils can also make good use of portable tape recorders for interviewing, and this can lead to a great deal of interesting and fruitful follow-up work.

Communications on the ground

There is much scope for the study of communications on the ground, not only in pure history syllabuses but also in integrated courses.[25] In combined studies it is often a good idea to start by analysing the present communications system of the district and to work backwards in time, using the comparative method. For history syllabuses the 'line of development' approach or the 'patch' method are also suitable. In all cases both map work in the classroom and fieldwork will involve study of the basic physical factors affecting the communications of the area—the use made of valleys, passes, ridges, fords, for example. Maps, too, may indicate the physical existence of historical evidence of past forms of communications—such as turnpike toll houses, disused railway lines and stations, and old canals, and these can be searched out in the field. The lines of Roman roads and turnpikes can also be followed on the ground. Construction techniques in railway and canal building, such as locks, embankments, bridges and tunnels, are often best appreciated by direct observation. Much of this is, of course, the stuff of industrial archaeology, and this has been shown to have great interest for children. The field observation of bridges, locks, station buildings, old company notices, toll houses, milestones and the like can form the basis for a great variety of valuable work, lending itself especially to the making of plans, sketching, photographs, descriptive writing, and later to modelling. Visits to transport museums, of which there are several round the country, and contact with railway preservation societies can reinforce a study of this kind.

There are, too, many opportunities for a combination of map and document work in the classroom with fieldwork in studying the effect of canal, rail and road development on the physical growth and structure of towns. Among suitable topics are the development of suburbs and commuter villages, the growth (and perhaps decay) of industrial development based on proximity to a canal or a railway station, and the linking of an inland town with the sea, but teachers will find others applicable to their own district. Often such communication studies can be undertaken in conjunction with the general study of historical topography (Chapter 4).

Battlefields and buildings

Where important battlefields are close enough to a school to be visited and are not obliterated by more recent developments they form a natural basis for historical fieldwork. There is, however, little point in the study of battles out of context of the war or campaign of which they formed a part, or of such topics as, for example, the weapons and nature of warfare of the period. Visits should therefore take place at an appropriate place in the syllabus and be preceded not only by map work but, in the case of secondary pupils, by a study of the battle from primary or secondary written sources. Teachers will find it helpful for themselves as well as their pupils to provide for a visit sketches of the various stages of the battle and a sheet of basic information. This will need some considerable preparation on behalf of the teacher, for the reconstruction of battles of the past is often a difficult matter. He will need to consult detailed works[26] and probably to simplify these to suit his particular class. On the site the source of the battle can then be traced, and such matters as the effect of the terrain on strategy deduced and discussed. With both younger and older pupils dramatic work can be undertaken on the spot if sufficient preliminary work has been undertaken in class.

In the study of architecture fieldwork is essential, and since most history teachers will certainly at some time wish to deal with the architectural features of buildings of one sort or another, there is clearly much scope for such activity. Sometimes purely architectural study will be the purpose, sometimes the study of the architecture of particular buildings will be part of more general work. Here it will be convenient to offer a few remarks on the use of fieldwork in the overall study of abbeys, castles, churches, stately homes and other dwellings, embracing within that their architectural features.

Any investigation at secondary-school level of social life from early modern times, and particularly in the eighteenth and nineteenth centuries, can hardly ignore consideration of the life style of the landed gentry, and in most parts of the country there are suitable stately homes open for inspection. A single visit at an appropriate time in the syllabus may be useful, but better is a series of visits each for a specific purpose. Such visits can be interspersed with work in the classroom and library, project activities benefiting from the interaction of literary search and observation on the ground. The archives of families connected with some great houses may be available in print in the publications of record societies or in the original in local record offices. In such cases the opportunity for combining the study of selected documents with a study of the house itself should not be overlooked. Such records as estate maps, building accounts and inventories go well with work in the field.[27] Many great houses have extensive grounds, which provide the possibility of integrated fieldwork embracing geography and biology.[28] Historical topics for group work include furnishings, interior decoration, heating and lighting, china, firearms, paintings and sculpture, the family and other occupants, life in the house in its heyday, servants, architectural features and the architects, building materials, comparison with other great homes, outbuildings and stables, landscape gardening, agriculture, the effects of the establishment on the village or villages in the neighbourhood, and perhaps its present significance as a tourist attraction.

Medieval monasticism and the Dissolution are frequently taught. Even adults however, find it difficult to appreciate the wealth and power of the abbeys in their heyday without viewing their physical remains, of which there are many.[29] For children an understanding of the organization of monasteries and the daily life of the monks is much easier when they see the physical layout. In some places, as at Chester, former monastic buildings have become incorporated into existing cathedrals, and these will form a complement to numerous derelict remains. Reasons for the siting and planning of individual monasteries,[30] the growth of the buildings at different periods, and the effects of the activities of the monks on the local topography (clearing forests, draining marshes, constructing and diverting water-ways) can be properly studied only on the ground, naturally in combination with map work and perhaps photographs.[31] As with visits to other buildings, study of good guidebooks (such as those published by HMSO) before the visit is essential for both teacher and pupil. On the spot useful tasks can include identifying main and outer buildings, recording their size, position, nature, relationship to each other, dates of construction and details of architectural style, and general observation on the site itself, including water supply, type of terrain, and so on.

A great deal of similar work is involved in the study of castles. Fieldwork helps a proper understanding of such matters as siting, the functions of the different parts of the building, the relationship of architectural design and style to defensive considerations, and the military practices and resources of the medieval period. Preliminary recourse to guidebooks or other authoritative works[32] will again be needed, and those providing plans or aerial photographs[33] will be particularly useful. Work in class may include a study of the nature of various types of castles, aspects of military architecture, and of contemporary forms of attack and defence. An introduction to the general history of local castles will then be needed, paying attention to the significance of their geographical position and perhaps their place as part of a larger military structure (as the Edwardian castles of Wales). With such background children can be required in the field to identify from plans provided the main parts of the buildings, military and residential; the chief features, like gates, keeps, towers, barbicans, moats, wells, wards or baileys, dungeons, different kinds of wall; the minor military features, such as merlons, embrasures, portcullises, posterns, arrow slits, machicolations, murder-holes and drawbridges; and domestic buildings, including the great hall, tower rooms, kitchens, bakehouses and garderobes. They can note the types of building material, the use of natural rock and the contours of the land, and the construction of artificial earthworks. Sometimes the earthworks of more ancient, simpler castles are visible, as at Berk-hamstead and Pickering, and these can be used to illustrate stages of development. Older children can record by sketches and diagrams the interlocking nature of defences, how tower covers tower and intervening walls, the reasons for the structure of the barbican, the purpose of concentric walls and central keep, and so on. They can investigate the siting of the castle, noting from inside and at a distance what can be seen from the towers, and how much of the surrounding countryside can be dominated and the problems of attack as well as defence. Evidence of the main purpose of the castle can then be sought and noted—as to protect the entrance to a harbour or dominate a plain. In some places, as Conway and Exeter, the castle forms part and parcel of the town defences, and the castle, town walls and gates will need to be studied as a whole for a true understanding.[34] Another theme to be covered is the domestic arrangements. Here pupils can be required to search out and record details of water supply, sanitation, living and sleeping accommodation for the family and the garrison, the chapel, and the provision of kitchens, storehouses and cellars, bakehouses and brewhouses, and their relationship to refectories and the great hall.

In some parts of the country, particularly in the Midlands, there are earthwork mounds which are all that survive of the so-called adulterine castles erected, originally as timber structures, during the troubles of Stephen's reign. These may be worth investigating if this period of history is taught. So too may the remains of moated homesteads found in, for example, Essex, Cambridgeshire, Suffolk, Lincolnshire, the East Riding and the west Midlands, and often marked on OS maps. They were associated with forest clearance in times when such protection was necessary.[35]

Churches and chapels provide visual illustrations for a variety of topics studied in school. Ancient churches give a clue to the location of the original nucleus of towns, for early settlements tended to cluster around them. The ages of the older churches in a town, deducible in part from architectural features and information displayed in the buildings, often illustrate the physical expansion of the town and indicate where former villages have been swallowed up or where the establishment of Victorian and more recent suburbs has required new churches. The buildings can, of course, be used to demonstrate styles of ecclesiastical architecture, but both churches and their surrounding graveyards can also demonstrate aspects of general local history and be linked to it. Thus the great fifteenth-century perpendicular churches in some parts of the country testify to the local prosperity of the wool trade at that time; monuments,

memorials and tombs in some churches may demonstrate the dominance in the locality of certain landed families, or perhaps the presence
of a prosperous trading or industrial community. Study of such
relics can be used with junior and younger secondary-school pupils to
lead to biographical work on important local figures and the general
context of their lives. Tombstones and the like, including effigies and
stained-glass windows, can be used to throw light on the social
structure of the past or on more elementary matters such as the study
of costume. The prevalence of infant and child mortality, the size of
families, the effects of epidemics, the impact of war (especially that
of 1914–18), all ascertainable from written records, can sometimes be
brought home to children more forcibly from memorials and grave-
stones, and here there is scope for note making, sketching and (with
permission obtained) brass rubbing. It may be that in some places
the church still bears the marks of treatment at the hands of Puritans
in the seventeenth century. Guidebooks or information displayed in
the building may indicate the existence there of a school—perhaps
the original town grammar school. The use of the tower in times past
as a look-out, a stronghold, or with its bells as a warning of invasion,
can be understood by seeing the tower from the inside.

Many secondary-school children rarely go to church and thus find
great difficulty in understanding the significance of that religious
strife which was so significant at various times in the past. Visits
to existing Anglican, dissenting and Roman Catholic churches and
chapels can help to give meaning to the religious controversies of
the past and to illustrate at a simple level differing religious outlooks,
for disputes over altars, vestments, prayer books, ornaments, stained
glass, statues and so on mean little to children to whom such things
are merely words.

A deeper understanding of religious matters is to be obtained, too,
through knowledge of the physical structure of churches and their
contents. Both junior and older pupils learn quickly by following on
the spot simple plans provided by the teacher, or by being required
to complete such plans themselves. If they have not visited other
churches they will usually need guidance in picking out such items
as a misericord, a piscina, a pyx, a sedilia, a squint, a tympanum or
a corbel, and external features like flying buttresses and gargoyles,
and they should be encouraged to build up glossaries of such terms.
In subsequent visits there can be detective work aimed at the identification and recording of these items. Appreciation of different styles
of ecclesiastical architecture and their relation to the periods of

construction will require continuing work in the classroom, but there is much scope, too, for identification in the field and recording by means of sketching, photographing, collecting postcards and the completion of work sheets or the compilation of personal or group booklets.[36] Also worth investigating are the materials used in building local churches and their relation to local resources, periods of construction and architectural style.

Attention should not be confined to one Anglican church; several local parish churches should be examined. Dissenting and Roman Catholic chapels will also be worthy of investigation, particularly at times when pupils are studying such topics as the Reformation, the emergence of the Puritan sects and the Methodist revival. Nonconformist chapels are unlikely to provide as great a scope for fieldwork as individual Anglican churches of any antiquity, but they do often demonstrate by their very plainness something of the nature of the belief of the sects to which they belong. Particularly worth undertaking as a class exercise (to indicate, for example, the strength and variety of Protestant Nonconformity in Victorian Britain) is a survey of such places of worship in a town or country area, involving also preliminary work with maps and directories, and perhaps reference to the religious census of 1851 (Chapter 7). It may be instructive, too, for pupils to seek out the size of present congregations comparing them with those in 1851 (taking into account population changes), and also to track down chapels now used for secular purposes.

Domestic buildings offer much opportunity for fieldwork. In a town or village a survey of houses of different periods can illustrate the area of original settlement and the extent and direction of physical growth at different periods. This can reinforce classroom work with maps and other records. With guidance, surveys can be undertaken by older juniors as well as secondary pupils and may vary from sampling different areas in a large town to noting every house or group of houses in a village. Sketching and perhaps photography will play an important part in recording, but with older pupils the more disciplined approach of compiling record cards summarizing different aspects of individual buildings can be worth while.[37] Such surveys can be undertaken without entering the houses, but if access is possible an examination of the internal structure of some older houses will be valuable. As with churches, building materials are an appropriate field of study related to the wider topic of regional variations in vernacular architecture. Here some comparison of the styles of the locality with those in other parts of the country is desirable, and all such study requires work in the classroom as well as on the ground.[38]

Such surveys can also throw light on past social conditions. The size of a house and its grounds gives a clu : to the status of the original inhabitants. Sometimes evidence of former use for domestic industry—as with the large windows of weavers' houses—can be detected. Pupils can learn to recognize the types of town housing used by different social classes at different periods, and to observe the effects on house style of changes in building techniques, rising land prices, and the advent of the motor car. The number and size of rooms in working-class houses, sanitary arrangements, means of heating and cooking and so on can be compared with those in middle-class houses.

There is obvious scope for linking historical with present-day social studies by comparing the children's own houses with those of the past, and by contrasting the original and present use of older properties. More complex fieldwork can take the form of a social survey of a street, investigating the occupations and family sizes and contrasting these with historical evidence from directories or census materials.[39]

Follow-up work

Fieldwork must be connected not only with sound preliminary work but also with follow-up work in the classroom, the nature of which will vary according to the situation. Some suggestions, however, are made in this section and the next. It is often advisable for follow-up work to be undertaken in three stages—immediate, intermediate and long-term. On the same evening as an expedition or the next day older pupils should make a fair copy of their field notes, sketches and other recordings, filling them out from memory. Younger children will need to talk about the trip and their findings as soon as possible, and for them and for less able seniors verbal discussion can form the immediate stage. Discussions will also be needed for all other pupils, too. The teacher should attempt to draw out an oral summary of the main findings from individuals and groups, at the same time rectifying misunderstandings, making good any omissions, and answering queries. This preliminary consolidation of the fieldwork while the experience is still fresh should soon be followed by decisions on future work and the compilation of a list of questions or topics which require further investigation.

The intermediary stage can take various forms. A common procedure is to make a class record of what has been discovered by compiling, by groups or as individuals, booklets concerned with different aspects of the study comprising descriptions, sketches, photographs, postcards, cuttings or copies of extracts from guidebooks, and so on. Some teachers find it useful to construct special work cards for the organization of such activities. An alternative, perhaps to be preferred for younger children, is to make a class display of such material. This may also include large-scale maps of various kinds to indicate the general site, and, where applicable, plans of buildings, as well as graphs, histograms, photographs and drawings. More senior children may prefer to make a series of specialized displays of different aspects of the fieldwork, for example devoting one entirely to a photographic record of changing styles of domestic architecture in a town, with accompanying descriptions and plans. With older children some personal record is also needed, since fieldwork must be seen as a natural part of the historical themes and topics being studied in class, to be integrated with those in their history files. With younger children history can be linked with craft and art work in following up fieldwork by the construction of simple or more complex models. Usually older children will have less time for such activities, but the co-operation of art and craft teachers may make such work possible, and in certain cases pupils studying technical drawing can adapt their skills to the construction of plans. If enthusiasm has been aroused, however, many pupils will be willing to spend lunch hours and after-school time on this sort of activity. The construction of film strips is another activity older pupils can undertake from transparencies taken on the spot, interspersed with captions and diagrams.

Imaginative work stimulated by visits to evocative sites such as abbeys, castles and battlefields can include dramatic activities, 'contemporary' diaries, letters, accounts and descriptions, and also creative art work. Some teachers encourage extempore dramatic work in the field following discussion of the sort of events that might have occurred there—as, for example, in a chapter house or a dungeon. Follow-up work in such cases could take the form of the production of a more polished version of the playlet. Where oral recording has been undertaken in the field this can be used as the basis for an imaginative or documentary 'broadcast', or, in conjunction with a series of slides or overhead projector transparencies, a home-made videotape recording. Sometimes those interviewed can be persuaded to visit the school to talk more generally to the class as a whole.[40]

In the long term further classroom studies may derive from fieldwork, following such recording and stimulus work as suggested above. It would, however, be artificial to distinguish too finely between intermediate and long-term activities. For the display and note-book work just described recourse to books of reference may well have been necessary. Long-term work is an intensification of this, where pupils build on the first-hand knowledge and experience they have acquired by further study of the topics concerned. Other forms of local evidence can be examined and information on similar sites or buildings taken into account, and the relation of the local to the national picture studied.

Again, local fieldwork may serve as an introduction to more general studies. Thus field study of a Welsh castle might lead to an examination of the role of defensive architecture in British history generally, to a series of lessons on medieval warfare, or to a study of Edward I's reign, or, if the syllabus was geared to local history in its own right, it might lead into a study of Anglo-Welsh relationships in this period and the effect of the building, say, of Caernarvon castle on the town and district. Field surveys of local churches could be followed by the construction of a time chart to demonstrate when the different sects were actively building places of worship. Comparison with present-day religious affiliation could branch out into comparative religion. The opportunity for a lead into religious or social studies in such cases is clear. Where co-operation with English teachers is possible or a 'humanities' syllabus exists, then clearly the reading of certain literary works and historical novels will sometimes be worth connecting with field visits. And, of course, where fieldwork in history or environmental studies is part of an external examination syllabus, careful personal records of visits (with objectives, procedures and findings carefully noted) and of the follow-up work will be needed.[41]

Archaeology
Teachers of history generally, and of local history in particular, cannot afford to be ignorant of archaeology, and though some will embrace it more enthusiastically than others and wish to pursue it in greater depth, all should make themselves generally familiar with its objectives and techniques, and with archaeological remains in their area.[42] Some regions are richer in the remains of certain historical periods than others, and this will naturally affect what the teacher will stress. If he intends to pursue the subject with senior secondary-school pupils he would benefit from attending adult classes and summer schools, or at least joining the local archaeological or

7 A school party helping to excavate Sandal Castle, Wakefield

historical society, for such societies usually organize lectures by experts and visits to sites. He will find useful, too, contact with local museums which not only house finds from local excavations but may have active field departments.

Archaeological excavations should be undertaken only by or under the supervision of experts. There is, of course, some demand, especially in the summer holiday months, for students and sixth-form pupils to assist in a humble way with excavations; and occasionally it may be possible for younger children to do a little such work (as washing pottery, or even trowelling).[43] At Sandal Castle, Yorkshire, for example, 1,500 children over nine years assisted in excavations revealing by 1973 the motte, moat and steep defensive sides of the fortress which had been destroyed in the Civil War. There will not often, however, be suitable work in a locality for children to join, and however attractive to children and teachers, we must recognize that practical archaeology, requiring skill or hard physical labour and a great deal of time (much of it not productive of any visible return), is hardly appropriate for inclusion as a regular part of the syllabus. But since archaeological exploration is one of the chief means by which the local history of early times is revealed it can hardly be ignored by teachers anxious to make their pupils aware of the history of their own region; and if purely national history is being taught, local archaeological examples will be equally valuable there. Children must, therefore, be made aware of the nature of archaeology and the techniques used by archaeologists, and they must be familiarized with the fruits of such activities in as many ways as possible.

There are a number of ways in which this can be done. For older secondary pupils 'archaeology' might be regarded as a substantial section of the history syllabus. It can be of special interest to academic sixth-formers, and at least one GCE board offers it as an A level subject. Its outward-looking nature and its novelty may also make it attractive to less academic school leavers of fifteen to sixteen who find much classroom history boring. Though actual digs may be out of the question, teachers can treat the history of archaeological discovery, archaeological terminology, the training of archaeologists and the work of ancillary technicians such as draughtsmen and photographers. Methods and techniques can be studied, too, including the use of maps and aerial photographs, prospecting equipment, surveying methods and instruments, excavation tools and methods, recognition of materials (timber, burnt wood, fabric, vegetation, food remains), and means of dating objects and deposits. Then the procedures followed with buildings and other remains uncovered can be studied, and, with smaller portable objects, sorting, packaging, analysing, conservation, restoration and display. Attention may be given, too, to the types of recording adopted, including perhaps writing up, drawing conventions for sites and objects, and something of statistical techniques.[44] The particular problems of rescue or emergency archaeology, undertaken when important finds are accidentally uncovered and time to investigate is short, and of underwater archaeology can perhaps be touched on, if local examples exist. Since archaeology is related not only to history but to other disciplines, such as geology, botany, zoology, medicine and anthropology, while the pure sciences also contribute, there are opportunities for team teaching.

In such study the locality should be used to supply as much

illustration as possible of all these matters, and where local history is being studied in its own right the connection of archaeological and other evidence—such as place names—exploited. Obviously this will involve visits to established sites, to sites being excavated (where often, given notice, field archaeologists will be willing to explain what is going on)[45] and to museums, not only to see the public displays but perhaps some of the work undertaken behind the scenes preparatory to display or preservation. The interrelationship between archaeological activities and the museum for teaching purposes is very strong.

Talks by local experts—professional and amateur archaeologists, museum curators and their staffs (including technicians)—may be arranged. In this, local archaeological societies may be willing to help. Some have junior sections where the individual may pursue the subject further. At least the school library should procure a set of the published transactions of these societies or offprints of suitable reports and articles. Where important sites exist in the area there will, of course, be monographs available, as, for example, the HMSO publications for sites controlled by the Department of the Environment.[46]

Sometimes small groups of seniors may be able to help with excavating or prospecting, but there are other useful activities concerned with archaeology which are suitable for school fieldwork. Pupils may, for example, make photographic collections of aspects of different types of local sites or of different kinds of finds uncovered —and these could include both freshly discovered objects and those already in museums. Where emergency excavations are being undertaken such help may be welcome so long as not too many children are involved on the actual site. Similar work might be done by children whose skills lie in the direction of sketching, while others might make scale plans and drawings. If class time cannot permit this, school archaeology or history societies may make it part of their activities. As well as visiting sites and museums and sketching, recording and describing—on which a great deal of work by juniors upwards can be based—children can make their own school collections, including original items (for it is surprising what some parents and grandparents can provide), and secondary material too—postcards, pictures, diagrams, plans, distribution and other maps, and sketches and photographs made by the pupils. Some school museum services will lend facsimile artefacts, or even originals. Models can be borrowed or purchased, but in most cases it will be preferable for pupils to make their own. These can be of several kinds: those portraying sites and buildings as they now exist; those where a reconstruction of the original is attempted; and those of small objects, which can sometimes be life-size.

Some archaeologists favour the furtherance of understanding of ancient buildings by attempting to reconstruct them.[47] An example of this 'experimental archaeology' is the erection of a huge 'Roman' granary at Lunt fort, near Coventry. The Avoncroft Museum of Buildings in Worcestershire has on its site old buildings rescued from demolition and re-erected, but has attempted, too, to build from scratch some 'Iron Age' huts and to experiment with the storage of grain in pits by methods thought to have been used. Such projects can be emulated in a humble way by children, especially in the junior school. They can attempt to grind corn to make flour, to make pottery by hand, or to reconstruct a Stone or Bronze Age hut.[48] Art and handwork can be involved in such projects, and children can be encouraged to base dramatic or other imaginative work on their own reconstructions or on visits to actual sites.

Many of the activities already described earlier in this chapter, such as the siting of buildings and settlements, can be applied to ancient remains, too. The sort of work suggested for archaeology generally applies equally to medieval archaeology, certain special aspects of which—deserted villages, moated sites, medieval buildings like castles and abbeys, and vernacular architecture—were also considered earlier. An even more recent arrival—industrial archaeology—is opening up a vast field of enquiry and study. It has been defined as 'recording, preserving in selected cases, and interpreting the sites and structures of early industrial activity, particularly the monuments of the industrial revolution'.[49] With greater concentration in school history syllabuses on economic, social and local history, there is great scope here, for in most areas there are physical remains of this sort. Factories, mills, bridges, aqueducts, canals, docks, railways, mines and quarries are all embraced by industrial archaeology, as well as major items of machinery and perhaps railway engines, buses, trams, coaches, carriages, cars, bicycles and the tools used by different craftsmen. Many such items have been traditionally found in museums, and now we have specialized museums devoted to rural life, folk craft and transport. Visits to these will be invaluable when aspects of the economic social or geographical history of the region are being studied.

Those aspects of industrial archaeology devoted to preservation and restoration and to recording what is likely to disappear lend themselves to specially interesting activities, particularly for the middle and upper forms of secondary schools. The scope for recording by photographs, drawings, measured plans, sketches and written descriptions is vast and in some areas too great a task for adult industrial archaeologists to cope with. Here pupils can indeed carry out original work of permanent value, attractive not only to academic fifth and sixth formers but to those school leavers who find little satisfaction in normal school work. Many skills are involved, and the variety of follow-up activities in terms of reading and project work is considerable. For A level economic history industrial archaeology has an obvious value, and since science and technology is usually involved it is a useful ingredient of fifth- and sixth-form 'general studies' courses, bringing differently orientated pupils and staff together.[50]

So diverse and common are the subjects of industrial archaeology that the objection to practical work by amateurs that attaches to the archaeology of early periods does not apply to the same degree. Enthusiastic groups or school societies can well undertake or assist in the restoration of a mill or a particular piece of machinery. Moreover there is great scope for connected oral history in interviewing and recording older persons who can give information about the construction or machine being studied. Finally industrial archaeology has a special value in the teaching of younger children. While time-consuming, it lends itself, like most fieldwork at that age, to an integrated approach to study involving not only local and general history but geography, English, mathematics and science. Art and craft can play a part, too, for many of the objects of industrial archaeology lend themselves as well to model making as do medieval castles.[51]

For notes to this chapter see pp. 172–5.

Bibliographical notes and references

Some general works: local history and archives

Emmison, F. G., *Archives and Local History* (1966).
Everitt, A., *New Avenues in Local History* (University of Leicester, 1970).
Finberg, H. P. R., and Skipp, V. H. T., *Local History: Objective and Pursuit* (Newton Abbot, 1967).
Hoskins, W. G., *Local History in England* (1972 edn.).
Rogers, A., *This Was Their World* (1972).
Stephens, W. B., *Sources for English Local History* (Manchester, 1973).
Tate, W. E., *The Parish Chest* (Cambridge, 1960 edn.).
West, J., *Village Records* (1962).

Some general works: teaching

Ballard, M., *New Movements in the Study and Teaching of History* (1971 edn.).
Burston, W. H., *Principles of History Teaching* (1963).
Burston, W. H., and Green, C. W., *Handbook for History Teachers* (1962; 2nd edn. 1972).
Chinnery, G. A., *Studying Urban History in Schools* (Hist. Assoc., 1971).
Douch, R., *Local History and the Teacher* (1967).
Dunning, R., *Local Sources for the Young Historian* (1973).
Fines, J., *The Teaching of History in the U.K.: A Select Bibliography* (Hist. Assoc., 1971).
Schools Council, *Humanities for the Young School Leaver: An Approach through History* (1969).
Watts, D. G., *Environmental Studies* (1969).

Other works are cited in the subsequent notes. For works on archaeology and fieldwork, see p. 172; on buildings, pp. 173–4; on industrial archaeology, p. 175; on museums, p. 173; on palaeography, pp. 40, 165.

Many useful articles are to be found in the journals *Teaching History* (abbreviated in the following notes to *T.H.*) and the *Amateur Historian* (now the *Local Historian*) (abbreviated to *A.H.*; *L.H.*). Only some of these are noted in the following pages.

Chapter references and notes

1 Local history and its value in school (pp. 1–14)

1 Price, M., 'History in danger', *History* 53 (1968).
2 Burston, W. H., *Social Studies and the History Teacher* (Hist. Assoc., 1954; reprinted 1967).
3 Everitt, *New Avenues in Local History*, 6–7.
4 E.g. Board of Education, *Handbook for . . . Teachers . . . in Elementary Schools* (HMSO, 1905), 63; Board of Education, *Teaching of History in Secondary Schools* (HMSO, 1908); Hist. Assoc., *Teaching of Local History* (1908).
5 In *Teaching of Local History*, 10.
6 Firth, C. B., *The Learning of History in Elementary Schools* (1929), 161.
7 Burston, *Principles of History Teaching*, 96.
8 See Douch, R., in Ballard, *New Movements*, 106 and works cited by Douch.
9 Burston, *Principles of History Teaching*, 95–6.
10 Hawkes, J., *Prehistoric and Roman Monuments* (1951), 1; McKisack, M., *History as Education* (inaugural lecture, Westfield College, London University, 1951).
11 This cannot be elaborated here, but see Watts, D. G., *The Learning of History* (1962): Hallam, R. N., in Ballard, *New Movements*; Fines, J., 'Recent research', *T.H.* 1 (2) (1969); Thompson, D., 'Some psychological aspects of history teaching', in Burston and Green, *Handbook for History Teachers* (1972 edn.); and works cited in all these.
12 Carpenter, P., *History Teaching: the Era Approach* (Cambridge, 1964), 33–4; Fines, J., 'History in school', *History* 53 (1968).
13 For successful examples see Schools Council Working Paper 48, *Environmental Studies, 5–13: Use of Historical Resources* (1973), 18.

2 Theoretical and practical problems (pp. 15–30)

1 Burston, *Principles of History Teaching*, 95–6.
2 See Rogers, V. R., *The Social Studies in English Education* (1968), 125–7.
3 Bantock, G. H., 'Discovery methods', in Cox, C. B., and Dyson, A. E. (eds.), *Black Paper Two: the Crisis in Education* (1968), 116. Cf. Ogden, C. K., and Richards, I. A., *The Meaning of Meaning* (1923), 216.
4 Hallam in Ballard, *New Movements*; Coltham, J., 'Junior school children's understanding of some terms commonly used in the teaching of history', Ph.D. thesis, Manchester, 1960.

5 For a penetrating criticism of the overemphasis of 'discovery' methods see Entwistle, H., *Child-centred Education* (1970), chapter 8.
6 Ausubel, D. P., *Educational Psychology: a Cognitive View* (New York, 1969), 498. For a survey of the research literature see chapter 14 of this work, and Ausubel, D. P., and Robinson, F. G., *School Learning* (New York, 1969), chapter 16. See also Ausubel in Fenton, E. (ed.), *Teaching the New Social Studies* (New York, 1966).
7 Bryant, M., 'Documentary and study materials, III', *T.H.* 2 (5) (1971).
8 Finberg and Skipp, *Local History*, 116.
9 *Cf.* West, J., *History Here and Then* (1966), 36, 48; IAAM, *Teaching of History* (1957 edn.), 187. For examples of extended periods devoted to local history in junior and secondary schools see Douch, *Local History and the Teacher*, 166–7, 193; West, *History Here and Now*, 59, 80–3.
10 Schools Council, *CSE: the Place of the Personal Topic—History* (1968); Docking, J. W., 'History and the CSE', *T.H.* 1 (4) (1970); McGivern, F. P., 'An approch to archives and local history', *ibid.* 2 (5) (1971); Holder, E., 'Industrial archaeology', *T.E.S.*, 2 June 1972.
11 *Cf.* Jones, R. B., 'Oakham School Mode III History O Level', *T.H.* 2 (7) (1972); Jones, J. A. P., 'Maidstone G.S. Mode III History O Level', *ibid. Cf.* Watson, J. B., 'A level without recriminations', *ibid.* 1 (4) (1970), 298.
12 But see Lawton, D., Campbell, J., and Burkitt, V., *Social Studies, 8–13* (Schools Council, 1971); Johnson, S., 'History and geography—an experiment in integration', *T.H.* 3 (10) (1973) (for a syllabus involving much local history).
13 See, for example, Goodson, I., 'The role of history in an urban study', *T.H.* 3 (10) (1973).

3 Preparing to teach local history (pp. 31–45)

1 Bibliographical aids include: Gross, C., *Bibliography of Municipal History* (2nd edn. 1966); Martin, G. H., and McIntyre, S., *Bibliography of British and Irish Municipal History*, 1, *General Works* (1972).
2 Pugh, R. B., (ed.), *Victoria History of the Counties of England: General Introduction* (1970).
3 Good introductions include Chapman, S. D., and Chambers, J. D., *The Beginnings of Industrial Britain* (1970); Chambers, J. D., and Mingay G. E., *The Agricultural Revolution, 1750–1880* (1967); and the Economic History Society's series 'Studies in Economic History'.
4 For towns covered see bibliographies cited in n. 1 above. For indexes see Stephens, *Sources for English Local History*, 6.
5 See most recent Royal Commission on Historical Manuscripts, *Record Depositories in Great Britain*; or Emmison, *Archives and Local History*, 10–21.
6 See also Latham, R. E., 'Coping with medieval Latin', *A.H.* 3 (1956–7).
7 Other helps include: Newton, K. C., *Medieval Local Records: a Reading Aid* (Hist. Assoc., 1971); Rycroft, A., *English Medieval Handwriting* (University of York, 1971); Emmison, F. G., *How to Read Local Archives, 1550–1700* (Hist. Assoc., 1967); Rycroft, A., *Sixteenth and Seventeenth Century Handwriting* (University of York, 1969).

8   White, S., *et al.*, 'Local history—a consumer research report', *History in School* 1 (Leeds History Teachers' Group, 1973). Of the class the majority preferred work on transcribed documents rather than originals.

9   See West, *Village Records*, 176–86; Richardson, J., *The Local Historian's Encyclopaedia* (New Barnet, 1974).

10 Photographic Ordering Section, Public Record Office, Chancery Lane, London WC2A 1LR.

11 Periodic lists appear in *Teaching History*. See also Bryant M., 'Documentary and study materials for teachers and pupils', *ibid.* 1 (3) (1970); Fines, J., 'Archives in school', *History* 53 (1968).

12 See Bolwell, L., and Lines, C., 'Resources for local studies: primary and middle schools', *T.H.* 2 (8) (1972).

13 Evans, K., 'Multi-media resource centres: a cautionary note', *Secondary Education*, June 1970.

14 See *School Library Resource Centres* (Library Assoc., 1970); West, J., 'The development of a local resources centre', *T.H.* 2 (7) (1972) (for a description of a centre and the equipment needed).

4 Local history in its own right: I (pp. 46–65)

1   E.g. Stenton, F. M., *Introduction to the Survey of English Place Names* (1925); Reaney, R.H., *The Origin of English Place Names* (1960); Cameron, K., *English Place Names* (1961); Copley, G. J., *Names and Places* (1964 edn.). See also Hoskins, W. G., *Fieldwork in Local History* (1967), 77 ff, and, for a useful list of place-name elements for juniors, Pluckrose H., *Let's Use the Locality* (1971), 67–8.

2   For such work with nine- to eleven-year-olds see Schools Council, *Environmental Studies*, *5–13*, 14–16.

3   In *Freedom and Authority in Education* (1952), 198–9, reproduced by permission.

4   Obtainable from the Ordnance Survey or the Geological Museum, South Kensington. For a full list see *OS Map Catalogue, 1974.*

5   Schools and public libraries can buy sets at a discount from the Ordnance Survey, Ramsey Road, Maybush, Southampton SO9 4DH.

6   See Chinnery, *Studying Urban History in Schools*, 22–3.

7   For the following paragraphs see Harley, J. B., *Maps for the Local Historian* (National Council of Social Service, 1972), 20 ff.

8   Emmison, F. G., 'Estate maps and surveys', *History* 48 (1963); Baker, A. R. H., 'Local history and early estate maps', *A.H.* 5 (1961–2); West, *Village Records*, 67–9.

9   See Bond, M., *The Records of Parliament: a Guide for Genealogists and Local Historians* (1964).

10 See Nunn, G. W. A., *British Sources of Photographs and Pictures* (1952). The Royal Photographic Society is preparing a *Directory of British Photographic Collections*: information from National Photographic Record, 66 Duke Street, Darlington.

11 For aerial films taken after 1966: Air Photo Cover Group, Ordnance Survey (address, n. 5 above). For previous years: Air Photography Officer, Department of the Environment, Prince Consort House, Albert Embankment, London SE1 7TF, or, for Scotland, the Registrar, Central

Register of Air Photography of Scotland, Scottish Development Department, York Buildings, Queen Street, Edinburgh EH2 1HY. Other collections include: University Collection of Air Photographs, Cambridge. The largest commercial collection is that of Aerofilms Ltd, 4 Albemarle Street, London W.1. Local newspapers, local planning departments and local photographic firms are also sometimes willing to lend or sell photographs to schools. See also Aerofilms Ltd, *The Aerofilm Book of Aerial Photography* (1965 edn.). The Department of the Environment maintains a Central Registry of Air Photography and can supply names of commercial companies which can provide photographs.

12   For some good ideas see Exwood, J. E., and Unwin R. W. (eds.), *Yorkshire Topography: a Guide to Historical Sources and their Uses.* (Leeds University, 1974).

13   The census schedules (or enumerators' books), 1841 to 1871 (below, pp. 89–92), provide information on the occupants of each house.

14   For detailed examples with young children see Newton, E. E., 'An Evertonian spilling over', *T.H.* 1 (4) (1970), 249 ff; Hopper, E., and Blyth, J. E., 'Model making as an approach to local history in the middle school', *ibid.*, 158 ff.

15   Gray, William, *Chorographia: or, a Survey of Newcastle-upon-Tine* (Newcastle, 1649), also in *Harleian Miscellany* 3 (1809), 276.

16   *Reports on Parliamentary Boundaries of Counties and Boroughs, 1831–32,* xxxviii; *Report on Boundaries of Certain Boroughs, 1837,* xxvi–xxviii; *Report of Local Government Boundary Commission,* 1888, li.

17   See 'The old road of England' in Randal, H. J., *History in the Open Air* (1936).

18   Simmons, J., 'Railway history in county records', *Jnl. of Transport History* 1 (1953–4); Hadfield, C., 'Sources for the history of British canals', *ibid.* 2 (1955–6); Duckham, 'Turnpike records', *History* 53 (1968); Stephens, *Sources for English Local History,* 98–104.

19   West, *Village Records,* for list of printed county maps.

20   Curnock N. (ed.), *John Wesley's Journal* (8 vols., 1909–16), 7, pp. 378–9.

21   Published by David & Charles. Fraser, R., *General View of County of Devon* (1794, reprinted Porcupines, Barnstaple, 1970).

22   Printed in Thomas, A. L. (ed.), in *Collections for a History of Staffordshire,* William Salt Arch. Soc., 1934 (1935), 51–2. Reproduced by permission.

23   Printed in Brown, A. J. F. (ed.), *English History from Essex Sources, 1750–1900* (Chelmsford, 1952), 53. Reproduced by permission of Essex C.C.

24   Salis, H. R. de (comp.), *Bradshaw's Canals and Navigable Rivers of England and Wales (1904)* (reprinted 1928, and Newton Abbot, 1969). For published records on turnpikes see West, *Village Records,* 160–1.

25   Bradshaw's guides for 1887, 1910 and 1938 were reprinted by David & Charles, 1968 and 1969.

26   For such a study and ideas for exercises with juniors see Wheeler, S., 'Young children, documents, and the locality', *T.H.* 1 (3) (1970).

27   Blyth, J., 'Archives and source materials in the junior school', *ibid.* 1 (1) (1969), 26.

28 See, for example, Milligan, H., 'The photographic aspect of industrial archaeology', *Industrial Archaeology* 1 (1964–5).

29 Gregor, H., 'Canals in the classroom', *T.H.* 2 (5) (1971), 21–3.

5 Local history in its own right: II (pp. 66–92)

1 From Morris, C. (ed.), *The Journeys of Celia Fiennes* (1948), 246–7, a good edition of her writings.

2 See Cox, E. G., *Reference Guide to the Literature of Travel* 1 (1935); Fussell, G. E., *Exploration of England: Select Bibliography of Travel, 1570–1815* (1955); Mayne, L. B., 'Tourists of the past', *A.H.* 3 (1956–8).

3 Pp. 220–422 give coastal shipping statistics, 1709–51, for eighty ports: potentially useful for class exercises.

4 Moens, W. J. C., *The Walloons and their Church at Norwich, 1565–1832* Huguenot Soc. of London 1 (1887–8), 220–1, quoted by permission.

5 See Woodward, D., 'Freemans' rolls', *L.H.* 9 (1970).

6 Rowe, M. M., and Jackson, A. M., *Exeter Freemen, 1266–1967*, Devon and Cornwall Record Soc., Extra ser., 1 (1973), 104, reproduced by permission.

7 Carus-Wilson, E. M., and Coleman, O., *England's Export Trade, 1275–1547* (1963).

8 Carus-Wilson, E. M. (ed.), *The Overseas Trade of Bristol in the later Middle Ages*, Bristol Record Soc. 7 (1937), 252 (revised edn., Martin Press, 1967), reproduced by permission.

9 From the Public Record Office, Chancery Lane, London WC2A 1LR. First check in a reference library: PRO, *Descriptive List of Exchequer, Q.R., Port Books, 1565–1700* (1960), and appropriate volumes of the List and Index Soc. series. See also, Woodward, D. M., 'Port books', *History* 55 (1970).

10 For an example see Goodson, I., 'The role of history in an urban study', *T.H.* 3 (10) (1973).

11 Aikin, J., *A Description of the Country from Thirty to Forty Miles round Manchester* (1795, reprinted Newton Abbot, 1969), 573–4.

12 For availability of these records see Jarvis, R. C., 'Sources for the history of ships and shipping', *Jnl. of Transport History* 3 (1957–8), 221–3. Permission to view, to HM Customs, King's Beam House, Mark Lane, London EC 3.

13 For such work with sixth-formers see Douch, *Local History and the Teacher*, 188–9.

14 Barrat, D. M., 'Glebe terriers', *History* 51 (1966).

15 From Gretton, R. H. (ed.), *The Burford Records* (Oxford, 1920), 674. Di = a half; di unius = half of one. Reproduced by permission of Oxford University Press.

16 A list is in Lord Ernle (Prothero, R. E.), *English Farming Past and Present* (ed. Hall, D., sixth edn., 1961), pp. xcix–c.

17 Young, A., *General Report on Enclosures* (1808; reprinted New York, 1971), 267. Other works include *A Six Weeks' Tour through the Southern Counties* (1768); *A Six Months' Tour through the North of England* (1770); *A Farmer's Tour through the East of England* (1771)—all also in later editions.

18 For a key to the volumes where the essays are to be found see Ernle (n. 16 above), pp. cii–ciii.

19 For the most useful see Powell, *Local History from Blue Books*, 22–4.

20 See Stephens, W. B. (ed.), *Sources for the History of Population and their Uses* (Leeds University, 1971), 8, 20–1 (*q.v.* also for Tudor and Stuart lay subsidies, another possible source for school use, and for many ideas for pupils' work on population sources generally).

21 Hoskins, W. G. (ed.), *Exeter in the Seventeenth Century: Tax and Rate Assessment, 1602–99*, Devon and Cornwall Record Soc., n.s., 2 (1957), 41, reproduced by permission.

22 See Ashmore, O., 'Inventories as a source of local history', *A.H.* 4 (1958–60), 157–61, 186–95; West, *Village Records*, 92.

23 Cash, M. (ed.), *Devon Inventories of the Sixteenth and Seventeenth Centuries*, Devon and Cornwall Record Soc., n.s., 11 (1966), 60–1, reproduced by permission.

24 For a list of places for which they exist see *Fifth Report of the Historical Manuscripts Commission* (1876). Some have been published.

25 For examples see Goodson, I., 'The role of history in an urban study', *T.H.* 3 (10) (1973); Stephens, *Sources for the History of Population*, 50–1.

6 Local history to illustrate national history: I (pp. 93–111)

1 Useful is Fisher, J. L., *A Medieval Farming Glossary: Latin and English* (National Council of Social Service, 1968).

2 Darby, H. C., *The Domesday Geography of Eastern England* (Cambridge, 1971 edn.); Darby, H. C., and Campbell, E. H. J., *The Domesday Geography of South-east England* (Cambridge, 1962 edn.); Darby, H. C., and Finn, R. A. W., *The Domesday Geography of South-West England* (Cambridge, 1967); Darby H. C., and Maxwell, I. S., *The Domesday Geography of Northern England* (Cambridge, 1962); Darby, H. C., and Terrett, I. B., *The Domesday Geography of Midland England* (Cambridge, 1971 edn.). See also Finn, R. Welldon, *The Norman Conquest and its Effects on the Economy, 1066–86* (1971), topographically arranged.

3 For ideas see Stephens, *Sources for the History of Population*, 44–5; Gosden, P. H. J. H., and Sylvester, D. W., *History for the Average Child* (1968), 75–7.

4 Douglas, D. C., and Greenaway, G. W. (eds.), *English Historical Documents, 1042–1189* (1968), 882.

5 See Latham, R. E., 'Inquisitions post mortem', *A.H.* 1 (1952–4).

6 From Duby, G., *Rural Economy and Country Life in the Medieval West* (1968 edn.), 459–60, reproduced by permission of Edward Arnold Ltd. The original Latin version is published in Stapleton, T. (ed.), *Chronicon Petroburgensi*, Camden Soc., o.s., 47 (1849), 157 ff—not too difficult for a teacher with basic Latin and a medieval word list.

7 Clough, M. (ed.), *Estate Surveys of the Fitzalan Earls of Arundel*, Sussex Record Soc. 67 (1969), 37 ff.

8 Page, F. M., *Wellingborough Manorial Accounts*, Northamptonshire Record Soc. 8 (1936), p. xiv, reproduced by permission of the society and Queens' College, Cambridge. A daywork was four perches, ten dayworks a quarter of an acre.

9   For ideas see Stephens, *Sources for the History of Population*, 45.

10 From Bland, A. E., Brown, P. A., and Tawney, R. H., *English Economic History: Select Documents* (1914), 66, 70–2, reproduced by permission of G. Bell & Sons.

11 For an example of such a playlet see West, *History Here and Now*, 23–4.

12 Ballard, A. (ed.), *British Borough Charters, 1042–1216* (Cambridge, 1913); Ballard, A., and Tait, J. (eds.), *British Borough Charters, 1216–1307* (Cambridge, 1923;) Weinbaum, M., *British Borough Charters, 1307–1660* (Cambridge, 1943).

13 Many are calendared in volumes of the Historical Manuscripts Commission. See also Tupling, G. H., 'Borough records: common council minutes', *A.H.* 2 (1954–6).

14 Twemlow, J. A. (ed.), *Liverpool Town Books, I, 1550–71* (1918), 283: slightly altered.

15 See works in n. 2 above.

16 Gross, C. (ed.), *Select Cases Concerning the Law Merchant, A.D. 1270–1638*, 1, Selden Soc. 23 (1908), 91.

17 HMC, *Manuscripts of the Duke of Portland*, II (1893), 268–70. The volume contains descriptions of many widely distributed journeys.

18 Hudson, W., and Tingey, J. C. (eds.), *Records of Norwich* 2 (1910), 160.

19 For fuller ideas see Hopper, E., and Blyth, J. E., 'Model making as an approach to local history in the middle school', *T.H.* 1 (3) (1970).

20 For inventories and these tax records see pp. 83 ff.

21 Robinson, C. B. (ed.), *Rural Economy in Yorkshire in 1641*, Surtees Soc. 33 (1857), 26–7.

22 Ashby, A. W. (ed.), *The Poor Law in a Warwickshire Village* (Oxford, 1912), 175.

23 Douch, *Local History and the Teacher*, 185–6.

7 Local history to illustrate national history: II (pp. 112–36)

1   Cutlack, S. A. (ed.), *Gnossall (Staffs.) Records, 1679–1837: Poor Law Administration*, Staffordshire Record Soc. Collections (1936), 6–7, reproduced by permission.

2   See Tupling, G. H., 'Overseers' accounts', *A.H.* 1 (1952–4).

3   Webb, J. (ed.), *Poor Relief in Elizabethan Ipswich*, Suffolk Record Soc. 9 (1966), 104–5 (edited), reproduced by permission.

4   For examples, see Tate, *The Parish Chest* (1960 edn.), 231–5.

5   Eden, F. M., *The State of the Poor* (1797), 3 vols. (abridged version 1928, ed. Rogers, A. G. L., but original worth seeking in large libraries).

6. See Tupling, G. H., 'Constables' accounts', *A.H.* 1 (1952–4).

7   Lister, J. (ed.), *West Riding Sessions Rolls, 1597/8–1602*, Yorks. Arch. and Topographical Assoc., Record ser. 3 (1888), 39, reproduced by permission of Yorks. Arch. Soc.

8   Cutlack, *Gnossal Records*, 73.

9   For references see Powell, *Local History from Blue Books*, 36–7.

10 See Coleman, J. M., 'Guardians' minute books', *History* 48 (1963).

11 For Parl. Papers providing such information for many places see Stephens, *Sources for English Local History*, 65–6.

12 For information on local charities see *Victoria County History*, and Reports of the Charity Commissioners (Parl. Papers).
13 Reproduced in Gill, C., *Plymouth in Pictures* (Newton Abbot, 1968).
14 Stephens, W. B., 'The air raids of 1940-1', *V.C.H. Warwicks.* 8 (1969).
15 Clay, J. W. (ed.), *Yorkshire Monasteries: Suppression Papers*, Yorks. Arch. Soc., Record ser. 48 (1912), 72, reproduced by permission.
16 Printed in Edwards, A. C. (ed.), *English History from Essex Sources, 1550–1750* (Chelmsford, 1952), 8.
17 Healey, C. (ed.), *Bellum Civile: Hopton's Narrative of his Campaign in the West, 1642–4*, Somerset Record Soc. 18 (1902), 94, reproduced by permission.
18 Pafford, J. H. P. (ed.), *Accounts of the Parliamentary Garrison of Great Chalfield and Malmsbury, 1645–6*, Wiltshire Arch. and Natural History Soc., Records Branch, 2 (1940), 73, reproduced by permission.
19 Hall, J. (ed.), *Memorials of the Civil War in Cheshire*, Record Soc. of Lancs. and Ches. 19 (1889), 223, reproduced by permission.
20 Greaves, R. W. (ed.), *First Ledger Book of High Wycombe*, Bucks Record Soc. 11 (1946), 138, reproduced by permission.
21 Stephens, *Sources for the History of Population*, 30.
22 *Census of 1851: Religious Worship*, Parl. Paper 1852–3, lxxix.
23 For such a survey see Stephens, W. B. (ed.), *History of Congleton* (Manchester, 1970), 204–5.
24 See Read, D., *The English Provinces, c. 1760–1960* (1964), for leads into many of these topics.
25 Briggs, A. (ed.), *Chartist Studies* (1959), comprises a number of local studies.
26 See Cannon, J., 'Poll books', *History* 47 (1962).
27 Douch, *Local History and the Teacher*, 185. Helpful is Addy, J., *Parliamentary Elections and Reform, 1807–32* (1968).
28 For examples of records just described see Brown, A. J. F. (ed.), *English History from Essex Sources, 1750–1900* (Chelmsford, 1952), 66–101, 183–210.
29 For example, Edgington, D., 'Teaching history through the local school', *T.H.* 3 (12) (1974); and especially Unwin, R. W., and Stephens, W. B. (eds.), *Yorkshire Schools and Schooling* (Leeds University, 1976) for many examples of pupils' exercises.
30 See the bibliography: Wallis, P. J., *Histories of Old Schools* (Newcastle upon Tyne, 1966).
31 *Digest of Parochial Returns*, 1819, xix; *Abstract of Education Returns: 1833*, 1835, xli–xlii.
32 Useful here is Seaborne, M., *The English School: its Architecture and Organisation, 1370–1870* (1971).
33 See Vaughan, J. E. and Argles, M., *British Government Publications Concerning Education* (1968); Powell, *Local History from Blue Books*.
34 Also found for some schools in *Minutes* (or *Reports*) *Committee of Council on Education* (annual Parl. Papers from 1840).
35 For examples of such work see *Environmental Studies, 5–13*, 12–13; Douch, *Local History and the Teacher*, 173–5.
36 Original in Museum of the History of Education, Leeds University.

37   E.g. Axon, W. E. A., 'Documents relating to the Plague in Manchester in 1605', *Chetham Miscellany* 3, Chetham Soc., n.s., 73 (1915).
38   See Smith, H. J., 'Local reports to the General Board of Health', *History* 56 (1971).
39   Harley, *Maps for the Local Historian*, 18; Gilbert, E. W., 'Pioneer maps of health and disease', *Geographical Jnl.* 124 (1958) (especially for cholera maps); Chinnery, G. A., *Studying Urban History in Schools* (Hist. Assoc., 1971), 26–7.
40   See, for example, Goodson, I., 'The role of history in an urban study', *T.H.* 3 (10) (1973); Wheeler, K. S. (ed.), *Geography in the Field* (Leicester, 1970), 60–1.
41   Useful are Stamp, L. D., *The Geography of Life and Death* (1964); Howe, G. M., *National Areas of Disease and Mortality in the United Kingdom* (1963).

8 Fieldwork and archaeology (pp. 137–62)

General works

Archer, J. E., and Dalton, T. H., *Fieldwork in Geography* (1970 edn.).
Hoskins, W. G., *Fieldwork in Local History* (1967).
Beresford, M. W., *History on the Ground* (1957).
Corfe, T. (ed.), *History in the Field* (Leicester, 1970).
Martin, G., and Turner, E. (eds.), *Environmental Studies* (Leicester, 1972).
Wheeler, K. S. (ed.), *Geography in the Field* (Leicester, 1970).

Crawford, O. G. S., *Archaeology in the Field* (1953).
Dymond, D. P., *Archaeology and the Historian* (Hist. Assoc., 1967).
Ordnance Survey, *Field Archaeology: Some Notes for Beginners* (1963).
Smallcombe, W. A., *Archaeology for Young People* (1961).

1   See Salt, J., 'The integration of history', in Corfe, *History in the Field*.
2   *Cf.* Schools Council, *Society and the Young School Leaver* (1967); Geog. Assoc., *Geography and the Raising of the School Leaving Age* (1968); Wheeler, *Geography in the Field*, 131–41.
3   For a course with young leavers see Preston, G., 'The value of local history in the school curriculum', *T.H.* 1 (2) (1969).
4   *Cf.* Walton, J., 'Historical field studies in secondary education', *Forum* 1 (2) (1959).
5   *Cf.* Roots, D., 'An investigation into the use of fieldwork in history teaching', *T.H.* 1 (4) (1970).
6   *Cf.* Boon, G., 'Instant fieldwork', *ibid.* 2 (8) (1972).
7   Field Studies Council (17 Carlton House Terrace, London s.w. 1). *Information 1973*; Council for Environmental Education, *Directory of Centres for Outdoor Studies*; Geog. Assoc., *Centres for Field Study* (1969); Youth Hostels Assoc., *Youth Hostels for School Journey Parties* (1970).
8   Salt, J., 'Approaches to field work in the primary school', *T.H.* 1 (3) (1970), 174.
9   Bantock, G. H., 'Discovery methods', in Cox, C. B., and Dyson, A. E. (eds.), *Black Paper Two: the Crisis in Education* (1969).
10   But see Doncaster, I., 'Historical buildings, museums and sites', *Handbook for History Teachers* (1964 edn.), and various chapters in

Dilke, M. S., *Field Studies for Schools*, 1: *Purpose and Organisation* (1965).

11 See 'General works', p. 172. Corfe; Archer and Dalton; and Plumrose, H., *Let's Use the Locality* (1971), have bibliographies. See also, for example, Corfe, T. H., *et al.*, *History Field Studies in the Durham Area* (Durham, 1966).

12 There are many works on schools and museums: see especially Bryant, M. E., *The Museum and the School* (Historical Assoc., 1961); Barrand, J., 'Museums and the teaching of history', *T.H.* 1 (2) (1969); DES, *Museums in Education* (1971).

13 See, for example, Museums Assoc., *Museum School Services* (1967). The Association's group for educational services can be contacted at 87 Charlotte Street, London WIP 2BX. Useful annual publications: *Museums and Galleries in Great Britain* (Index Publishers, Dunstable); Museums Assoc., *Museums Calendar*.

14 See Layton, E., and White, J. B., *The School Looks Around: a Book for Teachers about Local Surveys* (1951 edn.); Simpson, C. A., *Making Local Surveys* (1951).

15 See Wheeler, *Geography in the Field*, 77.

16 *Cf.* Corfe, *History in the Field*, 22–3.

17 Wheeler, *Geography in the Field*, 64–5.

18 *Cf.* Dunning, *Local Sources for the Young Historian*, 5–6, 22.

19 Hoskins, *Fieldwork in Local History*, 117–30 (and, for dating stone walls, 130–4); Hooper, M. D., *Hedges and Local History* (National Council of Social Service, 1971); Hooper, M. D., 'Dating hedges', *Area* 4 (1970); Hooper, M. D., 'Historical ecology', in Rogers, A., and Rowley, T. (eds.), *Landscapes and Documents* (1974). *Cf.*, for other botanical work, Duddington, C. L., 'History from plants', in Corfe, *History in the Field*, 15–17.

20 67 Gloucester Crescent, London N.W. 1.

21 Teachers should read Allison, K. J., *Deserted Villages* (1970), *q.v.* for a bibliography. Fuller is Beresford, M. W., and Hurst, J. G., *Deserted Medieval Villages* (1971). See, too, Ordnance Survey, *Field Archaeology*, 126 ff.

22 For a detailed example see Wheeler, *Geography in the Field*, 65–7.

23 See Steel, D. J., and Taylor, L., *Family History in Schools* (1973).

24 *Cf.* Fevre, M. Le, 'Introducing history to young children', *T.H.* 1 (2) (1969), 94.

25 For an example of integrated work see Boon, 'Instant fieldwork'.

26 E.g. Burne, A. H., *The Battlefields of England* (1950) and *More Battlefields of England* (1952); Kinross, J., *Discovering Battlefields in Southern England* (n.d.) and *Discovering Battlefields in Northern England and Scotland* (1968); Woolrych, A. H., *Battles of the English Civil War* (1961); *Field Archaeology*, 135 (Civil War sites).

27 E.g. Preston, M., 'Archives at Dynham Park', *T.H.* 2 (8) (1972).

28 *Cf.* Williams, R., 'Stately homes: an opportunity for experiment', *ibid.* 1 (4) (1970).

29 See Gilyard-Beer, E., *Abbeys: an Introduction to the Religious Houses of England and Wales* (HMSO, 1972); *Field Archaeology*, 130–1; *Ancient*

Monuments and Historic Buildings (HMSO)—lists published guides; OS, *Map of Monastic Britain*.

30 For a detailed example see Wheeler, *Geography in the Field*, 73–5.

31 See Knowles, D., and Joseph, J. K. St, *Monastic Sites from the Air* (Cambridge, 1952).

32 See O'Neil, B. H. St. J., *Castles: an Introduction to the Castles of England and Wales* (HMSO, 1973); and individual HMSO guides.

33 Also Simpson, W. D., *Castles from the Air* (1966).

34 Useful is Turner, H. L., *Town Defences in England and Wales . . . 900–1500* (1970), topographically arranged.

35 See Hoskins, *Fieldwork in Local History*, 54–5, and *Local History in England*, 132; *Field Archaeology*, 122 ff; Emery, F. V., 'Moated settlements in England', *Geography* 47 (1962); Le Patourel, J., 'Medieval Moated Sites Research Group', *L.H.* 11 (1974), *q.v.* for the group's publications.

36 Useful are Braun, H., *Parish Churches: their Architectural Development in England* (1970); Eden, P., 'Studying your parish church—from the building', *A.H.* 7 (1966–7).

37 For use of such cards adapted for schools see Brunskill, R. W., 'A note on the identification of domestic architecture', in Dilke, *Field Studies*; Wheeler, *Geography in the Field*, 61–3.

38 There are many works on domestic architecture. See especially Smith, J. T., and Yates, E. M., *On the Dating of English Houses from External Evidence* (1972, reprinted from *Field Studies* 2 (5) 1968) (purchasable from Classey Ltd, 353 Hanworth Road, Hampton, Middlesex); Hall, R. de Zouche, *A Bibliography on Vernacular Architecture* (Newton Abbot, 1973); Brunskill, *Illustrated Handbook of Vernacular Architecture* (1971); Barley, M. W., *The English Farmhouse and Cottage* (1961) and *The House and the Home* (1963).

39 For detailed suggestions see Martin and Turner, *Environmental Studies*, 115–22.

40 For a visit by an old miner to an infants' school see *Environmental Studies*, 5–13, 7.

41 *Cf.* Schools Council, *The Certificate of Secondary Education: the Place of the Personal Topic* (1968); Corfe, *History in the Field*, 41–2.

42 See 'General works' above, and Council for British Archaeology, *British Archaeology: a Booklet* (1960). The following contain gazeteers of sites, regional bibliographies, etc: Hawkes, J., *Prehistoric and Roman Monuments in England and Wales* (1951); Thomas, N., *A Guide to Prehistoric England* (1960); Wood, E. S., *Collins's Field Guide to Archaeology in Britain* (1972 edn.) (suggestions for follow-up work); HMSO, *Ancient Monuments and Historic Buildings* (periodically revised).

43 Details of sites on which groups of children can be taken to work may be obtained from 'Young Rescue', via the Secretary, 'Rescue', 25a The Tything, Worcester.

44 For a brief introduction to all this see Celoria, F., *Archaeology* (1970); Wood, *Collins's Field Guide*.

45 Information on excavations in progress obtainable from current *Calendar of Excavations*, Council for British Archaeology, 10 Bolton Gardens,

London s.w. 5. Useful too are the Council's annual *Archaeology in Britain* and *Archaeological Bibliography*.

46 The Royal Commission on Historical Monuments, Fortress House, 23 Saville Row, London WIX IAB will provide National Monuments cards for specified areas—giving for each site a map reference, description and bibliography.

47 Coles, J., *Archaeology by Experiment* (1973).

48 *Cf.* Corfe, *History in the Field*, 18–19; Preston, M., 'A primary school project on the Stone Age', *T.H.* 2 (6) (1971).

49 See Rix, M., *Industrial Archaeology* (Hist. Assoc., 1967) (for a general outline and select bibliography); *Field Archaeology* 134–6; Major, J. K., *Fieldwork in Industrial Archaeology* (1975).

50 Symonds, R., and Shreeves, W., 'Industrial archaeology in the sixth form', *T.H.* 2 (5) (1971).

51 For an ambitious exercise see Mack, D. W., 'Industrial archaeology in the primary school', *ibid.* 3 (9) (1973).

Index